THE IF-YOU FORM

IN ISRAELITE LAW

SOCIETY OF BIBLICAL LITERATURE

DISSERTATION SERIES

edited by

Howard C. Kee

and

Douglas A. Knight

Number 15

THE IF-YOU FORM

IN ISRAELITE LAW

by

Harry W. Gilmer

_____

SCHOLARS PRESS
Missoula, Montana

THE IF-YOU FORM

IN ISRAELITE LAW

by

Harry W. Gilmer

Published by

SCHOLARS PRESS

for

The Society of Biblical Literature

Distributed by

SCHOLARS PRESS
University of Montana
Missoula, Montana 59801

THE IF-YOU FORM

IN ISRAELITE LAW

by

Harry W. Gilmer
Wesleyan College
Macon, Georgia

Ph.D., 1969
Emory University

Library of Congress Cataloging in Publication Data

Gilmer, Harry Wesley.
    The if-you form in Israelite law.

    (Dissertation series ; no. 15)
    Bibliography: p.
    1. Jewish law--Language. I. Title. II. Se-
ries: Society of Biblical Literature. Dissertation
series ; no. 15.
    Law   296.1'8'014   75-23136
    ISBN 0-89130-004-X

Copyright © 1975

by

The Society of Biblical Literature

Printed in the United States of America

Printing Department
University of Montana
Missoula, Montana 59801

K.
.G5

Acknowledgments

I am especially grateful to Professor Martin J. Buss for the initial inspiration to pursue this project and for wise counsel and encouragement along the way. I also thank my readers, Professors Frederick C. Prussner and J. Maxwell Miller, for their critical appraisal and helpful suggestions. Finally I thank my wife whose contributions extend far beyond typing the preliminary and final drafts.

Biblical References

English translations of Old Testament passages and numbering of verses employed in this study are based on the <u>Biblia</u> <u>Hebraica</u>, eds., R. Kittel P. Kahle, A. Alt, O. Eissfeldt, 3rd ed. Stuttgart (Privilegierte Wurttenbergische Bibelanstalt), 1937

TABLE OF CONTENTS

LIST OF TABLES

I.   INTRODUCTION

For some time now it has been customary to study not only the date and origin of the different laws of the Torah but also their style and form by applying to them the method of the examination of types of literature (Gattungen) begun in biblical studies by Hermann Gunkel. His method of approaching this material was based on the assumption that language develops certain definite forms which serve specific functions. The linguistic form is thus related to a certain "situation in life" (Sitz im Leben) out of which it has developed. The task of the gattungsgeschichtliche approach is to analyze the varied forms and determine their background and sociological function.

Among the problems for which no satisfactory solutions have been offered is the question concerning those laws which appear to combine characteristics of both the conditional formulations and the commands and prohibitions. These are the prescriptions which take the form of a conditional sentence and employ a second person form of address, the If-You formulations.[1] Briefly, the problem may be stated: first, do they form a) a separate recognizable category of law, b) a conflation of other types, c) subdivisions of other types, or d) a combination of these possibilities? Secondly, do they serve some particular function in Israelite law?

One of the first attempts to classify the laws according to types was offered by C. A. Briggs in 1897 in his The Higher Criticism of the Hexateuch.[2] The following paragraph is revealing with regard to his point of departure:

> In the preparation of the legal terms for the New Hebrew Lexicon . . . it became evident to me that these terms were not used capriciously merely as synonyms (i.e. debarim, mishpatim, mitzvoth, huqqim, and toroth), but that they had a literary history, and were used in the main with discrimination in different layers of legislation. I was next called upon to investigate afresh the entire Hebrew legislation in the preparation of lectures upon the ethics of the Old Testament. The result

1

of that study was evidence showing that there were distinct and persistent types of Hebrew Law representing difference of origination.[3]

While Briggs made no attempt to deal with the life-situation of the laws, he did deal with form. His discussion is based on categories of law recognized in the Old Testament itself, that is, debarim, mishpatim, mitzvoth, huqqim, and tôrôth.

Gunkel himself did not devote much energy to the study of legal Gattungen. His major contributions were in the area of religious lyrics and saga.[4] In his initial attempt to sketch the history of literary types[5] he notes a distinction between the categorical imperatives of tôrôth and the hypothetical form of mishpatim.

Hugo Gressmann, Gunkel's pupil and close associate, treated the Book of the Covenant and the Decalogue in Die älteste Geschichtsschreibung und Prophetie Israels.[6] Discussing the life-situation of the laws therein, he recognized a difference between civil and religious law not only in content but also in form. In religious law (tôrôth) the priest speaks in the name of Yahweh. He found the origin of this type in the priestly oracle and in the priestly legal guidance. He viewed the civil law, however, as deriving ultimately from the Code of Hammurabi by way of Canaanite culture.

The first extensive attempts to classify Israelite laws according to type were those of Anton Jirku and Alfred Jepsen.[7] The former introduced the distinction set forth by Koschacker between Gesetzeskodex, legal code, and Rechtsbuch, collection of laws. According to Koschacker, a legal code is drawn up by a compiler and harmonized on the basis of a preconceived plan, whereas a collection of laws is simply a collection of separate ordinances, unaltered by the compiler, devoid of any rational scheme.[8] Jirku postulated that those bodies of law in the Old Testament which had been identified through literary critical research (the Decalogue, Exod. 20:1-17 = Deut. 5:6-21; the Book of the Covenant, Exod. 20:23-23:19; the cultic decalogue, Exod. 34:10-27; the Schechem Dodecalogue, Deut. 27:15-26; the Holiness Code, Lev. 17-26; the Deuteronomic Code, Deut. 12-26) belong mostly to the category of _Rechtsbuch_. Only the Sinai Decalogue and the Shechem Dodecalogue are legal codes according to this analysis. The material which is before the investigator already displays a mixture of civil and religious provisions. The task of the form critic, therefore, is to look behind these secondary collections and try to piece together the original bodies of law (legal codes) from which the laws in the Torah ultimately derive.

Jirku starts from the premise (his "iron law"[9]) that all of the laws of a legal code drawn up by one author must be characterized by a unity of style and general expression. Using this criterion, he believed it possible to separate and regroup the ordinances and so to reconstruct the original codes of law, at least in part. He distinguished ten basic forms outside the strictly priestly legislation.[10] From this it would appear that there existed ten primitive legal codes from which the Old Testament legislation was extracted. He further argues that the compilers of the bodies of law in the Old Testament must have had before them varied legal codes from which they extracted laws which suited their purposes. They edited and harmonized to a certain extent, but they had lost the feel for stylistic unity and did not employ a single style for their collections.

Jirku was the first to set the laws in If-You style apart from other categories, separating even the singular If-Thou from the plural If-Ye. He distinguished the following different ways of formulating law:

1. „Wenn" (If) Formulation.[11] This style is introduced by the conditional kî, occasionally by _'im_ as in Exod. 21:23, followed by a verb and its subject. Secondary cases are introduced by _'im_.

2. „Du-sollst" (Thou-shalt) Formulation.[12] Laws in this style are prohibitions or commands cast in the second person singular imperfect.

3. „Er" (Relative) Formulation.[13] This form is introduced in the third person, often by _'îš_, _'îššah_, or _nepheš_ _'ašer_. They employ the third person singular imperfect and are found only in Lev. 20:2-21.

4. „Fluch" (Curse) Formulation.[14] Laws of this kind are in the form of a curse. All the Old Testament examples are in Deut. 27. They begin with _'arur_, followed by the subject against whom the curse is directed. An

example: "Cursed be he who removes his neighbor's landmark" (Deut. 27:17).

5. „Ihr-sollt" (Ye-shall) Formulation.[15] These are similar in form to those of the second category except that the command or prohibition is set forth in the plural.

6. „Jussiv" (He shall) Formulation.[16] Laws of this style are introduced by a verb in the third person singular or plural. The grammatical jussive is not always employed.

7. „Partizipial" (Participial) Formulation.[17] These are introduced by a participle replacing the conditional particle and verb of the „Wenn" formulation. The apodosis is short, always involving the death penalty.

8. „Wenn-Du" (If-Thou) Formulation.[18] In Jirku's opinion, this formulation results from the combination of the „Wenn" formulation and the „Du-sollst" formulation. It is introduced by the particle kî or 'im, but the second person singular is employed. The following are included in this category:[19]

```
Exod.  21:2-6
       22:24a
       22:25
       23:4f
Lev.   19:33a, 34b
       25:25
       25:35-37
       25:39-41
       25:47-52, 54
Deut.  15:7-10a
       15:12-14, 16-17
       17:2-5
       17:8-12
       17:14-16a, 17-20
       18:9-11a
       18:11b
       20:1, 5
       20:6
       20:7
       20:8
       20:10-14
       20:19f.
       21:1-4, 6-7
       21:10-14
       21:22f.
       22:6f.
       22:8
       23:10-12
       23:13f.
       23:25f.
       24:10-13
       24:19-21
```

9. „Wenn-Ihr" (If-Ye) Formulation.[20] This is similar to the „Wenn-Du"
formula except that the plural is employed. There are only two examples of
this form listed by Jirku, namely Lev. 19:23-25 (fruit trees) and Num.
35:10b ff. (Cities of Refuge).

10. „2. Wenn" (Second If) Formulation.[21] This particular style is similar
to the „Wenn" formulation except that the order of the conditional and the
subject is reversed. The sentence begins with the subject, ʾādam, nepheš,
ʾîš, or ʾîš ʾîš, followed by the particle kî, which may be continued then by
ʾim.

Jirku regrouped the laws of the Torah according to these ten categories
and found these to constitute reasonably coherent systems. According to his
analysis, the oldest are the „Wenn" and the „Du-sollst" formulations. He
assigned the „Wenn-Du" formulations to the first half of the period of the
divided monarchy on the basis of Deut. 17:14f., which is the law concerning
kingship. No attempt, however, was made to deal with the question of the
place of the laws in the life of the people.

One of the major problems relating to Jirku's analysis has to do with
his fundamental premise. Is there actually an iron clad principle such that
all laws of a legal code drawn up by one author must take the same form? In
his comparative study of other Near Eastern law codes, he has noted that
only the Code of Hammurabi is a genuine legal code (Gesetzeskodex). The
others (Lipit-Ishtar Code, Middle Assyrian Laws, and the Hittite Code), he
concludes, are compilations (Rechtsbücher). All of these, he asserts, are
drafted in precisely the same conditional style which is found in Hebrew
law. In addition, he introduces the Salic Law, the Napoleonic Code, and the
German Bürgerliches Gesetzbuch in support of his theory.

There is a considerable degree of homogeneity in the formulation of
Near Eastern law. A conditional style is employed for the most part.[22] On
the other hand, a more thorough study of the Near Eastern codes examined by
Jirku reveals many departures from stylistic uniformity. For example, both
the Code of Hammurabi[23] and the Hittite Laws[24] reveal such exceptions. So
it appears upon closer examination that Jirku"s "iron law" is not valid. All

one can actually affirm is a tendency to employ stereotyped formulas in the promulgation of ancient laws. One single law-giver or collector may utilize several types of formulations since form and content are so closely related. Content must certainly be regarded as having a part in regulating the way in which a law is formulated.

Soon after the appearance of Jirku's own work, one of his pupils, Hans-Helmut Krause, dealt with the categories of Israelite law in his inaugural dissertation.[25] His interest was in determining the sources of Deuteronomy. Arguing against Staerk[26] and Steuernagel,[27] who had published analyses of Deuteronomy based on the change from the singular form of address to the plural, Krause employed Jirku's theory of stylistic similarity in analyzing the material. In the Deuteronomic legislation he recognizes seven styles. These correspond to some extent with Jirku's classification, but there are several notable exceptions. The following are the seven forms which he recognizes:

1. Mi ha ˀîš (What-man).[28] These are the beginning words of a series located in Deut. 20:5-9. Jirku had placed these in his „Wenn-Du" category, believing them to have been originally in that form.[29] The ordinances in this section are spoken by the officers and deal with release from military service. This particular form occurs nowhere else in Deuteronomy. Krause believes the source to have been a book containing the law of the officers which originated in an early period when such unpractical ordinances were possible. He does not, however, offer any reason why they would have been possible in an earlier period and not later. Military exemptions are in fact practiced in modern times.

2. Deut. 14:1-21a (Ye-shall).[30] This second category is a series of regulations dealing with clean and unclean. They are characterized by the use of the second person plural imperfect, sometimes followed by the negative lō. The form corresponds to Jirku's "Ihr-sollt" category. This section in Deut. is not included in the latter's analysis since he does not include the strictly priestly legislation in his classification. Krause believes this group of ordinances to have come from Temple ordinances or

from a larger work containing cultic ordinances and other laws.

3. K̂î with 3rd person singular (If).[31] Unlike Krause's first two groups, laws in this group and the four remaining are found scattered through the Deuteronomic legislation. This particular form is roughly equivalent to Jirku's „Wenn" form. It should be noted, however, that Jirku places Deut. 21:1-9 in his „Wenn-Du" category rather than here as with Krause, who regards the second person forms as secondary. Krause sees these third person laws as old, originating in the justice of the city gate presided over by the elders.

4. K̂î with 2nd person singular (If-thou).[32] This formulation clearly falls under Jirku's „Wenn-Du" formulation. Krause, on the other hand, went beyond his teacher in his analysis of the Deuteronomic legislation by making formal distinctions within this general group. The first division he makes is between those forms which employ k̂î with the second person singular in the protasis, followed by a "Thou shalt" form in the apodosis ("If thou . . . , thou shalt . . ."), and those which employ k̂î plus the third person in the protasis followed by a "Thou shalt" form in the apodosis ("If he . . . , thou shalt . . .").[33] This is a valid distinction as will be seen below. Krause, however, does not find it very helpful and maintains that all of these laws are from one source.

One further distinction which he makes has to do with the tone of the laws, whether charitable (mild) or severe (streng).[34] Following Steuernagel, he points to the humanitarian character of the If-Thou styled legislation. As to the period of the composition of the code from which these laws were taken, he thinks it later than the period of the early divided monarchy. He compares the slave laws with the understanding reflected in Jer. 34:9ff. It is on this basis that he dates the composition of the If-Thou forms in the same period as that of Jer. 34:9ff. Krause apparently is as convinced of an "iron law" as is his teacher.

The following are included in this category:

Deut. 13:2-6
       13:7-12

8

```
Deut.    13:13-19
         15:7f
         15:12-18
         17:2-7
         20:1
         20:10-18
         20:19-20
         21:10-14
         21:22-23
         22:6-7
         22:8
         23:10
         23:11-14
         23:22-24
         23:25f.
         24:10-13
         24:19
         24:20
         24:21f.
         25:11-12
```

5. „Nicht sollst du."[35] This group begins with the negative lō and is
followed by the second person singular. Their contents include religious
and humanitarian laws. Jirku includes these short pregnantly styled laws
in his „Du sollst" group. Krause assigns them to a late period, but believes
they pre-date 586 B.C.

6. „Nicht soll er."[36] Formulations in this group begin with lō and are
followed by a prohibition in the third person singular. Krause remarks that
Deut. 19:15, the law concerning witnesses, in content borders on that of the
"If he . . . , thou shalt" formulation. „Nicht soll er" laws do not include the threat of penalties, and they are formulated in an impersonal
manner. Krause, on the basis of Deut. 24:16, relates this group to the time
of Jeremiah (see Jer. 31:29f.) and also to that of Ezekiel (Ezek. 18).

7. „Du sollst."[37] This is a group of short pregnantly styled prescriptions
formulated in positive fashion. Krause considers these laws, which are
cultic in nature, to have come from an early period. Following Hempel, he
locates them in the north.

In addition to these seven forms, Krause mentions the existence of
three other styles but does not discuss them--an imperative formulation; a
form beginning, "When Yahweh your God . . ."; and another beginning, "When
thou comest into the land . . ."[38]

Alfred Jepsen published a study of Israelite law the same year in which
Jirku's work appeared.[39] He attempts to determine the sources of the

Book of the Covenant. On the basis of form and content he sets forth four categories of law from which he believes its author has drawn:

1. "Hebrew mišpatîm."[40] These are case laws introduced by the particle kî or ʾim. They are cast in the third person. Jepsen includes examples in this category such as Exod. 21:2 in which the second person does appear, for he believes the second person to have been introduced by the compiler of the code. These "Hebrew mišpatîm," according to Jepsen, are the product of a settled society. He finds their origin among the Hebrews who were already settled in Palestine prior to the conquest.

2. "Israelite mišpatîm".[41] These laws are introduced by a participial verb and deal with capital offenses. The penalty is typically stated môt yûmāt. Jepsen points to the rhythmical character of these formulations. He also includes the maledictions of Deut. 27 together with these as parallel forms. These laws he regards as the peculiarly Israelite way of formulating law. They go back to a very early period, reflecting desert traditions.

3. Religious and moral prohibitions.[42] Laws of this style begin with lō followed by the second person imperfect and are rhythmical. The Decalogue is cast in this form. These prohibitions are Israelite in origin and were adopted early, in desert conditions. Jepsen points to the relationship between these laws and the admonitions of the wisdom tradition.[43]

4. Cultic regulations.[44] This group consists of humane and cultic prescriptions both Israelite and Hebrew in origin. They include both short commands and prohibitions in the second person singular imperfect. Unlike the religious and moral prohibitions these exhibit no rhythmical quality. Jepsen includes some If-You forms in this category (Exod. 20:25, 23:4 and 5); he considers these "mixed forms" to be the work of the editor of the sources. He believes the laws in this general group to rest on old traditions, and to have originated as a result of the interaction with Canaanite culture.[45]

In the same year, 1927, also Sigmund Mowinckel's work on the Decalogue appeared.[46] He shows how an individual group of laws, the Decalogue, might have come into existence. He considers the Decalogue as it presently stands to be late. The late date, however, does not apply to the literary type to which it belongs. He finds the origin of the Decalogue in the cult, specifically in a New Year and enthronement festival which, he thinks, had the function of a Covenant Renewal Festival.[47] He further states that during this festival a cultic prophet recited the Decalogue. He connects the decalogues with the interrogation of those attending the festival by the priests. The entrance requirements concerning ritual purity were recited by the priests at the entrance to the place of worship.[48] Such decalogues varied from place to place, so that there were more than one, each with its own background. As the form developed, its content was broadened and generalized to define in general terms what was required in order to belong to the covenant people. Finally, it came under prophetic influence.

The great merit of Mowinckel's work is that he seriously endeavored to get behind the literary sources to the origin of the law in the life of the people.

Another investigation which centered on the Book of the Covenant began to appear just a few years later. This was the study by Julian Morgenstern which began in the _Hebrew Union College Annual_ in 1928 and continued through 1932.[49] Morgenstern distinguished four different kinds of law in the Book of the Covenant on the basis of form and content.

1. The d^ebarim.[50] Prescriptions of this category are couched in concise, direct form. They employ the second person singular and may be either negative or positive. These prescriptions all have to do with some basic ritual principle, as in Exod. 23:12a. According to Morgenstern's analysis, ten of these d^ebarim formulated in the Northern Kingdom by Elisha and his followers formed the nucleus of the Book of the Covenant.

2. The mišpatîm.[51] This category is essentially equivalent in form to Jirku's „Wenn" formulations and Jepsen's Hebrew mišpatîm." They are laws which Morgenstern believes deal with matters of a civil nature. He, however, believes them to be of Israelite origin. As they appear in the Book of the Covenant they are only fragments of an ancient Israelite body of civil law. He further believes them to have been incorporated into the Book of the Covenant by secondary Elohist writers or editors.

3. The huqqim.[52] This is the term which Morgenstern applies to the participial formulations, Jepsen's Israelite mišpatîm. Morgenstern finds no
indication of the origin of this type of law in the Book of the Covenant
itself, whether it stems from judicial decision or from some other context.
It is found only in priestly legislation, although something approximating
it rather closely is found also in the Book of Proverbs.[53] According to
Morgenstern, the laws of this type derive ultimately from the post-exilic
ʿedāh, a predominantly priestly organization which, however, did have some
lay representation. This organization was presided over by the high-priest
and held forth in the inner court of the Temple.

4. The miswot.[54] Like the dᵉbarim, these laws are also couched in concise,
direct form employing the second person singular address. Morgenstern
observes that this form, more than the others, is frequently amplified by an
explanatory statement which gives the basis or justification for it. This,
along with their purely ethical subject matter, appears to set them off from
the dᵉbarim. No specific penalties are attached other than the disfavor of
the Deity.

It is clear that Morgenstern does not consider the If-You formulations
as a separate category. Where they occur in the Book of the Covenant they
fall among at least three of his classifications. In Exod. 21:2-6 and
21:14 he considers the "you" part to be editorial. Exod. 20:25, which contains an If-You formulation, is placed with the dᵉbarim. Several If-You
forms occur in the sections which he has designated miswot, namely Exod.
22:20-26, 23:1-9.

In 1934 Albrecht Alt sought to clarify the origins of Israelite law[55]
by applying the gattungsgeschichtliche method to the legal literature.[56]
Heretofore, Jirku had made a detailed analysis of the formal characteristics
of Israelite law and Jepsen had differentiated on the basis of form a
specifically Canaanite-Hebrew legal tradition and one specifically Israelite.
Neither, however, had examined the origins of the categories in the life of
the people. To this task Alt set himself. He distinguished two general
types of laws in the Torah, the so-called casuistic and the apodictic.

The casuistic laws are the impersonal conditional formulations,[57] which we have already seen in Jirku's „Wenn" classification, Jepsen's Hebrew mišpatîm, and Morgenstern's mišpatîm. The life situation of this type of legislation Alt concludes to be the work of the ordinary courts presided over by the family elders.[58] It is fundamentally secular in use and corresponds in terms of style and content to the ancient Near Eastern law codes. Alt warns, however, against looking too far afield for the origin of this law, for he believes that it was taken over by the Israelites from their Canaanite neighbors.[59] He believes it to have been the common possession of all of the Canaanite inhabitants of the land. The Israelite settlers adopted it for their own use, probably made some alterations, and finally it was incorporated into the Book of the Covenant, into Deuteronomy and also into the Holiness Code. Alt thinks that the way in which this law was cultivated and passed on was by way of a series of legal functionaries.[60] These were the so-called "minor judges" of whom we are told very little in the Book of Judges except that they judged the people for a certain number of years. In contrast to the "major judges" who were charismatic military leaders, these officials were "proclaimers of the law" similar to those in ancient Iceland who were responsible for the annual proclamation of the law and who served to adjudicate disputed cases.

The apodictic law is considerably different. It was brought by the Israelite settlers as they came in from the desert. Since it covered some of the same subjects as the Canaanite law, there was bound to be a period of adaptation in which the Israelites brought the two traditions together. Alt finds the confluence of the Canaanite casuistic law and a specifically Israelite legal form in Exod. 21:23-25 and in 21:13, 14, both of which contain If-You formulations. Here he sees an originally Canaanite casuistic formulation having been interpolated by the Israelite lex talionis.[61] These two examples, however, cannot be taken without qualification as purely Israelite legal forms. Alt believes he has found a purely Israelite form in a dozen terse prescriptions, all of which begin with a participle (Jirku's "Partizipial" formulation). The example given is Exod. 21:12 - "He who strikes a man so that he dies, shall be put to death." To this participial form Alt applies the designation "apodictic."[62] It is characterized by metrical structure, association in series, and formulation in the second person singular.

He includes in the apodictic category the commands and prohibitions ordinarily in the second person, including the curses of Deut. 27:15-26, the series concerning prohibited degrees of relationship in Lev. 18:7-18, a series in Exod. 22:17, 20, 21, 27; 23:1-3, 6-9 dealing with special categories of persons toward which actions must be guarded, and finally the Decalogue of Exod. 20 and Deut. 5 All of these laws express an unconditional prohibition and are animated by divine authority. As to the origin of apodictic law, Alt holds that "alles in ihnen ist vielmehr volksgebunden israelitisch und gottgebunden jahwistisch . . ."[63] Their origin is to be sought within Israel, and this not in the local secular courts but in the cultic life of the people. It is here that their imperative tone belongs and such absolute prohibitions could be imposed.[64] Alt cites the setting of Deut. 27 in which the Levitical priests delivered the curses orally to the people assembled near Shechem. The people were to respond to each curse with the cry "Amen!". From this Alt concludes that it was the duty of the Levites to proclaim the apodictic law.[65] He goes on to conclude that this action was not confined to one time or place but was repeated at the Feast of Tabernacles (the New Year's festival) every seventh year when the covenant was renewed.[66] Such public recitation would also account for the concise and metrical form of the apodictic formulas. Concerning the question of date, Alt believes the necessary conditions to have been present with the establishment of the common relationship with Yahweh and its formalizing in the Covenant.

It is clear that Alt does not recognize the If-You formulations as a separate category. At least two prescriptions in which a conditional formulation is accompanied by the second person he attributes to a conflation of casuistic and apodictic forms. In the slave law of Exod. 21:2, he believes the second person to be editorial. In the parallel law of Deut.

15:12 he attributes the second person to the stylistic proclivities of the Deuteronomist.

Alt's analysis has met with wide acceptance. W. F. Albright, who has differed with Alt on other points, enthusiastically endorsed the latter's treatment of law in his review.[67] The standard introductions have also generally employed Alt's distinction.[68] His theory, however, has not been without its critics. Sigmund Mowinckel questioned whether the use of the so-called apodictic law in the cult necessarily proves its cultic origin.[69] Benno Landsberger expressed doubt concerning Alt's distinction and suggested that the variation in forms might just as well be attributed to what he called "der lebendige Predigtstil".[70] I. Rapaport[71] and T. J. Meek[72] both attacked Alt's position on the basis of the existence of what they called apodictically styled prescriptions in the comparative Near Eastern legal material. These, as George Mendenhall later emphasized,[73] were cast in the third person rather than in the characteristic second person of the biblical style. Mendenhall went on, however, to show the existence of apodictic formulations in the Hittite treaties, thus again challenging Alt's position of the uniqueness of Israelite apodictic legislation. He cites this example from a treaty between the Hittite king Mursilis and one Kupantakal: "Thou shalt not desire any territory of the land of Hatti." He furthermore points out its similarity to the tenth commandment of the Decalogue. It is Mendenhall's opinion that there is a structural dependence of the Israelite covenant form upon these treaties.[74]

More recently, parallels to the Israelite prohibitions and commands have been recognized in two other spheres. Stanley Gevirtz locates them in West-Semitic curses,[75] and Rudolf Killian, along with others, has found parallels in Egyptian wisdom literature.[76]

Since the appearance of Joachim Begrich's essay, "Die priesterliche Tora",[77] it has been clear that cultic regulations are set forth in several forms. Begrich sought to clarify the meaning of the term tôrāh. He finds it originally to have designated the authoritative priestly instruction to the laity concerning what was clean and unclean, holy or profane. There is

15

little of this kind of instruction preserved in the Pentateuch, but Begrich does find examples of what he considers are imitations of such tôrôth in the prophetic books, such as Hag. 2:12 - "If one carries holy flesh in the skirt of his garment, and touches with his skirt, bread or pottage, or wine, or oil, or any kind of food, does it become holy?" The priests answered, 'No'. Within this earliest kind of tôrāh Begrich differentiated four types: 1) Commands and prohibitions which have an imperative character.[78] They are brief and are formulated in the second person plural,[79] and are represented as the word of Yahweh. He also included conditional sentences in this category (If ye . . . .).[80] 2) Declarations in the first person, by Yahweh, of things which please or displease him.[81] 3) Definitions of what is holy or profane, clean or unclean, set forth in direct form.[82] According to his analysis this is the most common form for such definitions.[83] 4) Definitions of what is holy or profane, clean or unclean, in relative style which set forth a consequence in direct form, sometimes in the second person, but mostly in the third.[84] The third type is related to the fourth, but differs in that it only declares what is clean or unclean, holy or profane, without indicating consequences.

Another major category distinguished by Begrich is the priestly dāāt.[85] This type, according to his analysis, is composed of regulations regarding the cult which are intended only for the priests. It composes a kind of professional science. Obviously, such knowledge would not be addressed to the laity. He includes the larger part of the cultic legal material preserved in the Old Testament in this category. It is impersonally formulated, for the commands and prohibitions in the second person plural are completely absent from this category, as well as the first person declarations of Yahweh. Several grammatical forms are employed, including the jussive, the imperfect, and the perfect consecutive.

Besides the reactions to Alt's analysis, there have appeared additional formal studies of Israelite law. In 1946 Henri Cazelles published a study of the Book of the Covenant[86] in which he attempts to categorize the laws therein under four headings:

1. Les _formules_ _casuistiques_.[87] This is the common style of the ancient oriental legislation and thereby the easiest to determine. Characteristic of this legislation is its practical nature and its dependence on previous legal tradition. Cazelles compares this style to that of the omens.[88] These, he finds, have "l'aspect le plur juridique."[89]

2. Les _formules_ _participiales_.[90] With Alt and Stoderl, Cazelles sees a close relationship between these participial formulations and the maledictions in Deut. 27. They are maledictions in which an equivalent expression has been substituted for the verb "to curse". Cazelles sees this substitution as a movement away from the magical connotations of the curse, particularly as held by the Egyptians.[91] While such formulas may be found in extra-biblical texts, he does not believe it necessary to look beyond the Old Testament for their origin.

3. Les _formules_ _en_ _style_ _direct_.[92] In this category Cazelles includes both the singular and plural series, essentially a combination of Jirku's „Du-sollst" and „Ihr-sollt" formulations. He concludes, however, that only the singular group merits the name "series." These are the laws in the second person imperfect which are found also in Lev. 18 and 19, in Deut., and particularly in the Decalogue. "C'est un ordre qui vise toute une categorie d'actes a eviter ou à accomplir."[93] These commandments are not temporally limited, thus the imperfect is used in preference to the imperative. Again, no foreign influence is found.

4. Les _formules_ _conditionnelles_ _en_ _style_ _direct_ (If-thou).[94] Cazelles does not consider laws in this style to have come from a code drawn up in unitary style. Rather, he takes them to be secondary combinations of the direct style and the casuistic style. They are all formulated in the singular. Their secondary character is evident, he believes, in Exod. 21:14 and 23, where the second person address does not appear until the apodosis ("If-he . . . you"). He has pointed to the parallels with the similarly styled admonitions of the Egyptian instructional literature.[95] He finds similarity in style but difference in thought.[96] In the wisdom admonitions it is a matter of success in life, while in the Book of the Covenant it is a matter

of respecting laws regulating human behavior. Thus the latter are more juridical, closer to the casuistic law than to the commandments.[97] Cazelles includes the following in this group:

> Exod. 20:25
> 21:2
> 21:14
> 21:23
> 22:23
> 22:24-26
> 23:4
> 23:5

The first two categories which Cazelles has devised are reminiscent of Jepsen's first two categories. His conclusions concerning the origins of the forms, however, are historically conservative as compared to those of the latter, for Cazelles traces all of the forms of the Book of the Covenant ultimately to Moses' promulgation of the law in the area of Kadesh-Barnea.[98]

One of the most important studies of the types of Israelite law since Alt's work is that of R. A. F. MacKenzie.[99] His treatment is extensive and thoroughgoing. While he maintains two large categories, casuistic and apodictic, the contents of these categories do not correspond to Alt's grouping. In addition, MacKenzie has introduced sub-classifications, to some degree reminiscent of Jirku's work, though he argues against the latter's theory of unitary style in the individual codes. He finds a relationship between the standard casuistic form of the Near Eastern codes and that of Israelite law but maintains that the legal system of Israel is "on the fringe" of this classification because of its highly religious character and because of the divine authority which stands behind it.[100] With regard to apodictic law, while the Egyptian royal decrees show general resemblances of style to the Israelite legislation, there is no need to look for any direct relationship. "If a precedent must be found, it would be more natural to look for it in the mode of expression of the _paterfamilias_, patriarchal head of a nomad family or clan, commanding or forbidding what seemed good or evil in his sight."[101]

MacKenzie divides the casuistic material into four forms:

1. The Standard Form.[102] This form is the oldest and most important of the casuistic formulations and is similar to that found in other Near Eastern

18

codes. These laws are "crystallizations of customary jurisprudence, drafted
as a guide for the use of judges, and completely secular in tone."[103] Unlike
Cazelles, MacKenzie does not find the origin of this casuistic legislation
in the law-giving activity of Moses nor in already established Canaanite
culture. Rather he reasons that this body of law originated among Hebrews
already in the land who had not been part of the Exodus tribes, but who were
related to them by blood.[104]

2. The Second Casuistic Form.[105] This form resembles the standard casuistic
form except that the kî ʾîš construction is simply reversed. It begins with
a nominativus pendens, usually ʾîš or ʾiššah, which is followed by a conditional clause and an apodosis in the third person which sets forth the
remedy for the case. This is similar to Jirku's „2. Wenn" formulation.
Laws in this category deal with basic crimes such as murder and blasphemy.
They have a rhythmic quality which suggests an oral promulgation. MacKenzie
concludes that these formulations are of great antiquity and may well be the
peculiarly Israelite version of casuistic law, even pre-Mosaic.[106]

3. The Relative Formulae.[107] This form begins with a relative clause introduced by a variety of relative formulas including ʾîš ʾašer, ʾiššah ʾašer,
ʾîš ʾîš ʾašer, nepheš ʾašer, kol nepheš ʾašer, ʾîš kî, ʾîš ʾîš kî, nepheš kî
and ʾadham kî.[108] MacKenzie regards these as a late and literary development in Israel,[109] growing out of the torah of the priests, defining that
which is clean and unclean.

4. Participial Forms.[110] This category consists of a small number of penal
laws which use a participial clause to set forth a case. The penalty imposed
is usually stated with the phrase môt yûmat. It will be recognized immediately that this is the same as Jirku's „Partizipial" formulation. Alt had
included these laws in his apodictic category.[111] MacKenzie places them
with casuistic law since they do not command a future action, but rather
indicate to the judges a penalty to be imposed. He identifies them as
"legal-religious principles"[112] and includes ten curses of Deut. 27 among
them.[113] They are one of the oldest forms and were framed for public recitation. Specifically, MacKenzie holds that they were created by Moses him-

self for the first ratification of the Covenant.[114]

In the apodictic law a demand is placed squarely upon the subject which regulates his future action. No provisions are made for breaches of such law since obedience is assumed. The following sub-groups constitute MacKenzie's apodictic class:

1. The Preceptive Imperfect.[115] This is a group of precepts in which the second person imperfect (both singular and plural)[116] is employed in the giving of the command. In addition, MacKenzie includes in this group certain jussive forms accompanied by the second person pronoun. He enumerates four points which characterize this law:[117] 1) it is true law, yet derives not from the community but from a superhuman authority, 2) it has an entirely categorical and unconditional character, 3) the imperative form ordinarily utilized for a command is abandoned in favor of the second person imperfect, and 4) the singular is predominantly used instead of the plural even though the law is addressed to the masses. The plural tended to replace the singular in later development. All subjects are covered by this type of formulation, religious, civil, cultic and ethical. MacKenzie believes this particular form to be the "direct outcome of Moses' religious experience."[118]

2. The Jussive Form.[119] This form is not to be confused with the grammatical jussive of personal commands. These laws rather are formed by the third person imperfect. The Jussive form sets forth a categorical command and is frequent in ceremonial legislation. It has a brevity of style. MacKenzie, finding support in I Sam. 30:24f. and in Deut. 24:16, locates the origin in royal law, in the early period of the monarchy.[120]

3. Mixed Forms (If-You).[121] He sees them as the result of a combination of the standard casuistic form with the second person address of the commandments. His basis for dividing laws of this category into two groups is different from Krause's, though for the most part the resulting groups are similar. MacKenzie has divided his material on the basis of whether the emphasis falls on the protasis (the casuistic element) or upon the apodosis (the "apodictic" element). In the former case, the protasis defines a legal case and the apodosis declares in direct style how the authorities are to

handle that case (usually, but not always equivalent to Krause's "If he . . .,
thou shalt . . ."). MacKenzie holds that these laws are the creation of the
Deuteronomic author. The second type, in which the emphasis falls on the
apodosis, includes a description of a future situation in the protasis, and
directs in the apodosis a future action to be performed or omitted. He holds
that laws of this type are more closely related in spirit to "apodictic" law
which places an obligation on the subject and maintains a strongly indigenous
creation of the Mosaic tradition,"[122] an early form of Mosaic tôrah. The
following are included in his two categories:

```
        First Mixed
            Exod.  21:14
            Deut.  17:2-5
                   17:8-13
                   19:1-6
                   19:11-13
                   19:16ff.
                   22:23-27
                   25:11f

        Second Mixed
            Exod.  20:25
                   21:2f
                   22:24a
                   22:25f
                   23:4,5
            Lev.   19:33f
                   22:29
            Deut.  15:7-10
                   15:12-15
                   15:16f
                   17:14f
                   21:10-14
                   22:6f
                   22:8
                   23:10
                   23:22f
                   23:25,26
                   24:10-13
                   24:19,20,21
```

While the formal distinction may be a valid one, the origins which
MacKenzie has attributed to these sub-groups are questionable. For example,
in the case of his first type, instructions to authorities, he has overlooked
the fact that such instructions also appear in the second person in other
literatures. Thus there is no necessity to attribute it to a Deuteronomic
genus litterarium.

In summary, it is evident that MacKenzie sees four categories emanating directly from the lawgiving activity of Moses, the Preceptive Imperfect, the Participial Forms, the Second Casuistic Form, and the Second Mixed Form. Three additional forms are seen as later, the Relative Form, which he believes developed late in the period of the monarchy, the Jussive Form, which he connects with early royal legislation, and the First Mixed Form, thought to be the work of the Deuteronomic author. Only the Standard Casuistic Form does he consider to be of foreign origin.

A detailed criticism of MacKenzie's work is not in order at this point. However, a few questions should be raised on the basis of his study. First, there remains some doubt whether the participial constructions are to be placed with the casuistic forms, with MacKenzie, or among the apodictic forms, with Alt, or in some other category of their own. Secondly, MacKenzie places more emphasis on the creative role of Moses in the formation of Israel's legal styles than is reasonable or necessary. This is not to discount Moses' central role in the history of Israelite legal tradition. However, far too much of the legislation contained in the four Mosaic forms seems to belong to a more settled way of life than would allow us to attribute to them an origin prior to Israel's existence in Canaan.[123] In addition, the Israelite tribes would have certainly had some legal traditions maintaining their tribal order prior to Moses.

Two other studies have given some recognition to the If-You formulations. Walter Kornfeld in his study of the Holiness Code,[124] closely following MacKenzie, refers to them as "Mixed Forms" and divides them into two groups on the same basis. In addition, he takes cognizance of the variation between singular and plural but considers it only a formal difference of little consequence. The first mixed classification he believes to be a more juristic character. He finds only one example in the Holiness Code, the law of the stranger (Lev. 19:33f.). In the second category he includes the following:

      Lev.   19:5-8
               19:23-25
               25:25
               25:35-37
               25:39-41
               25:47ff.

Christian Feucht's work on the Holiness Code[125] also recognizes a "mixed" category. Following Jirku he distinguishes within this category a „Wenn-Du" formulation and a „Wenn-Ihr" formulation. The former he believes to have originated in the preaching of the law by the Levites,[126] as already suggested by von Rad. The „Wenn-Ihr" formulation he considers unique in the Israelite texts and designates it as a priestly tôrāh which may have developed from the „Ihr-sollt" formulation.[127]

One result of the research which has been carried on during the more recent period is that Alt's "apodictic" classification is being more and more shaken. Not only is the uniqueness of "apodictic" law being questioned, but as we have also noted with regard to MacKenzie's classifications, the question is being raised as to what laws may be properly included in this category. For example, Hartmut Gese, in a short article,[128] would limit the apodictic designation only to those series of prohibitions which employ the second person. These apodictic formulations, he feels, belong either to the realm of worship or to that of the education of the Israelite men. He concludes that the participial forms are secondary and could not have been the original form of Israelite law.[129]

Recently, also Erhard Gerstenberger[130] has departed from the analysis of Alt as well as from the theory of a close relation between the apodictic formulations and the Near Eastern treaty form. He rejects Alt's definition of apodictic formulations since one is left with a number of sub-classes which lack unity both in form and in content.[131] According to Gerstenberger the formal criteria which Alt had set forth for apodictic law[132] will not hold the varied elements of the genuine Israelite law together since they are either too general or apply only to one sub-class of apodictic law. As to content, much of what Alt had included in his apodictic category really belongs to casuistic law, particularly the relative formulations and the participial constructions which also deal with legal cases and the remedies for those cases. Gerstenberger rejects the description "categorical" as applying only to apodictic law. All law is categorical in the sense that it expresses a legal sanction. The genuine "legal clauses" set forth a definition of a crime and what is to be its legal consequence. In contrast to such genuine "legal clauses" there are commands and prohibitions which do not set forth any legal consequence. They do not look back upon a crime which has been committed, but look forward in terms of warning. To this category, Gerstenberger gives the name "Prohibitive"[133] instead of "apodictic." The prohibitives have as their main subject rules for daily life which are for the most part formulated negatively. It is not necessary, however, to exclude constructions which are positively formulated since in content they too are prohibitive. With regard to the If-You formulations Gerstenberger has only a few observations.[134] He does not indicate that they form a separate category. Rather, he sees them as standing close to the "apodictic" formulations.

Gerstenberger finds examples of the prohibitive in the legal codes of the Old Testament (Book of the Covenant, Deuteronomy, Holiness Code, the Decalogues) and points to family regulations (such as Jonadab's instructions in Jer. 35:6f), the avowals of innocence (such as that in Ezek. 18), the Torah-liturgies, the prophetic threats and the wisdom sentences as related forms.[135]

He maintains that while the framework in which the prohibitives of the Decalogue are found may indeed be of cultic origin, this does not necessarily mean that the prohibitives themselves originated in a Covenant Renewal Festival.[136] According to his analysis, the styling of the prohibitions as the speech of Yahweh must be seen as secondary. The original authority behind them is to be sought in a patriarchal institution. Gerstenberger reaches the conclusion that the series of ten and twelve prohibitions in Lev. 19:1-18, Exod. 22:20ff., and Deut. 22-25, is a secondary theologizing.[137] They were originally grouped in smaller series of two or three, possibly even four. The development of longer series was necessitated by such practical needs as the instruction of youth, cultic and juridical usage. An examination of the Sinai narrative reveals no integral connection between it and the prohibitions.

Gerstenberger finds no direct relationship between the prohibitions and the Near Eastern treaties.[138] In the treaties the address of the prohibitions is particular; in the Israelite prohibition it is more universal. The conditions defined in the treaties are also particularistic, relating to the situation of one man, the vassal. In addition, the stipulations of the treaties are supported by sanctions which are missing in the Israelite prohibitions. The prohibitions exhibit no arrangement in series in the treaties.

Gerstenberger believes he has found the origin of the prohibitions in the instructional ethos of the patriarchal family order. He draws upon the role of Jonadab as leader of the Rechabites in Jer. 35, and his admonitions (vv. 6-7) as an example of such patriarchal instruction. The latter's commands reflect the ethos of the Rechabite clan. Also Lev. 18 is described as belonging to this clan ethos.

In further support of his hypothesis Gerstenberger turns to the Wisdom literature, where he recognizes two major forms, "instructions" formulated in direct address and "sentences" formulated in the third person.[139] He believes these differ in origin as well as in form, the instructions originating in the words of the father of a family. Both in the Israelite wisdom literature and in Ancient Near Eastern parallels Gerstenberger locates sufficient parallels in form and content to posit an old international clan ethos. From this point of origin the prohibitive was adopted into Israelite law, into cultic regulations and into the admonitions of the wise.[140]

Some general support for Gerstenberger's thesis is found in the work of two other scholars, George Fohrer and Wolfgang Richter.[141] Fohrer also recognizes a nomadic or semi-nomadic background for apodictic series. He distinguishes, however, between apodictic series which find their place in illiterate nomadic or semi-nomadic society, and apodictic style which includes several types and which belongs to the primitive forms of human speech. Thus while finding a relationship between apodictic law and the clan ethos, Fohrer would allow an origin there only for the series, while Gerstenberger finds the origin of the prohibitions themselves in the clan ethos. Richter's study deals with another Gattung, the admonition (Mahnspruch), which he finds common to both law and wisdom texts. He distinguishes the admonition from the prohibitive forms but traces them to closely related origins, the former to the formal instruction directed to officials and the latter to the formal instruction directed to the children of the official classes. Thus while he differs with Gerstenberger concerning the point of origin of these forms, he posits a similar connection between law and wisdom.[142]

From the foregoing survey it is apparent that many questions concerning the forms of Israelite law are as yet unanswered. At this point in the discussion, however, the following observations stand out: 1) Concerning the basic casuistic formulation of Near Eastern law there is greatest agreement. Its impersonal conditional style is well known, and it is surely related to the juridical proceedings of the Ancient Near Eastern courts. There remains some question concerning the period when this kind of law was taken up by Israel, and there remains the question which forms beyond the standard casuistic form may be included here. 2) The so-called apodictic law poses greater difficulties. It is no longer possible to speak of the uniqueness of apodictic law as Alt has defined it. The discovery of numerous Near Eastern parallels to the commands and prohibitions of Israelite law has opened up the question of the origin of this kind of formulation. A related question, and one receiving considerable attention recently, is concerned with the connection between law and wisdom. 3) It is clear that Alt's apodictic classification was too inclusive. In particular, the participial laws are not similar to the commands and prohibitions either in form or intent. They show some relation to the conditional forms with their definition of a legal case and its consequence. There remains a question, however, whether it belongs to a separate independent category. 4) Related to these problems is that of the laws which appear to combine characteristics of both the conditional formulations and the commands and prohibitions, the If-You formulations.

The basic thesis of the present study is that the If-You formulations in Israelite law are not a late mixture of types, but an old form which had been in use over a long period of time and which is clearly related to the commands and prohibitions. To demonstrate this thesis we have analyzed first the material in Old Testament historical, prophetic, and wisdom contexts which falls within the scope of the problem, second the If-You formulations in the legal portions of the Old Testament, and third the If-You formulations in ancient Near Eastern texts. Conditional constructions using the second person singular or plural are considered in this study in order to determine over as broad a base as possible just what kinds of expressions may take this form.

II.   IF-YOU FORMULATIONS IN OLD
TESTAMENT HISTORICAL, PROPHETIC, AND WISDOM MATERIAL

Among the speech patterns employed outside of legal materials, the
If-You formulation recurs with some measure of regularity. Three major
groups are readily distinguishable: If-You forms in narrative contexts,
If-You forms in prophetic speech, and If-You forms in wisdom. The first-
named group is rather general in nature while the second and third constitute special areas of concern. Can anything important for the use of If-You
formulations in law be determined through an investigation of the formal
structure of the formulations which occur in the non-legal portions of the
Old Testament? The seeming peculiarity of such formulations in law already
suggests that they may have been introduced into law from some other source
or that they represent law at a stage of development otherwise not well
known.

If-You Forms in Narrative Contexts

By far the largest number and variety of If-You formulations outside
the legal portions of the Old Testament occur within the context of narratives.[1]   Three questions may be applied to these formulations: 1) Who is the
speaker? 2) To whom is he speaking? 3) What is happening in this speaking?
The first two questions concern the context of the formulations. This is
not uniform as the following analysis will show. Such formulations come
from the lips of a variety of speakers and are addressed to a variety of
hearers. The third question concerns the content of the formulation. On the
basis of the three questions, five subdivisions can be differentiated: requests, agreements, threats and promises, counsels, and directives. These
may be further grouped into two categories on the basis of the presence or
absence of the imperative, either grammatical or intended.[2]   Requests and
directives contain an imperative, the others do not.

27

1. Conditional Demands

Requests. The formulations in this group set forth a straightforward, polite request. The request itself is a word spoken by a subordinate to one in authority. What is asked is not balanced off by any reciprocal promises as in the agreements, nor is there any threat implied should the request go unfulfilled. The following is an example of this kind of formulation: "If now I have found favor with thee, then show me a sign that it is thou who speakest with me" (Jud. 6:17b).

TABLE I. NARRATIVE REQUESTS

Ref.		Subject	Cond.	Num.	Speaker	Addressee
Jud.	6:17	Gideon's call	'im	sg.	Gideon	Yahweh
	6:36	the fleece	'im	sg.	Gideon	Yahweh
ISm.	27:5	David's residence	'im	sg.	David	Achish
IKg.	8:44-49	Solomon's prayer	kî	sg.	Solomon	Yahweh
ICh.	13:2	the ark	'im	pl.	David	Israel
IICh.	6:22-24	Solomon's prayer	'im	sg.	Solomon	Yahweh
	6:34	Solomon's prayer	kî	sg.	Solomon	Yahweh
Neh.	2:5	Jerusalem's plight	'im	sg.	Nehemiah	king

The protasis sets forth a condition under which the request would be considered. The condition itself may be either present or future. The protases envisioning present conditions are rather vague references to the speaker's having found favor in the eyes of the addressee.[3] The future conditions envisioned are specific situations to which the request applies. The request itself comes in the apodosis and is directed to one having authority. In most cases, Yahweh is the addressee. In two exceptions, I Sam. 27:5 and Neh. 2:5, the address is to royalty. In one other exception, I Chron. 13:2, Israel is addressed. In all of the request formulations appeal is made to the good nature of the addressee. It is by this route that the will of the speaker is transferred to the addressee.

Directives. The directive is a word spoken by an authority, usually to one in a subordinate position. In this respect, it stands at the opposite pole from the request. Its intent is to command the future course of action of the addressee under certain specified conditions. The will of the speaker is imposed directly upon the addressee. An example is Gen. 47:6b - "And if thou knowest any able men among them, then make them rulers over my cattle."

TABLE II. NARRATIVE DIRECTIVES

Ref.		Subject	Cond.	Num.	Speaker	Addressee
Gen.	15:5	offspring	'im	sg.	Yahweh	Abraham
	42:19f.	subterfuge	'im	pl.	Joseph	brothers
	47:6b	brothers	'im	sg.	Pharaoh	Joseph
Jos.	17:15	land	'im	sg.	Joshua	tribe
	22:19	altar	'im	pl.	Phinehas	Reubenites
Jud.	7:10	Midianites	'im	sg.	Yahweh	Gideon
	13:16	Samson's birth	'im	sg.	angel	Manoah
Ru.	4:4b	levirate custom	'im	sg.	Boaz	kinsman
ISm.	6:3	the ark	'im	pl.	priests	Philistines
	20:6ff.	David's flight	'im	sg.	David	Jonathan
	21:10	Goliath's sword	'im	sg.	Ahimelech	David
IISm.	15:33f.	Hushai's service	'im	sg.	David	Hushai
IIKg.	4:29	Shunammite woman	kî	sg.	Elisha	Gehazi
	9:15	Jehu's coup	'im	pl.	Jehu	people
	10:6	Jehu's coup	'im	pl.	Jehu	elders

In the protasis a condition or situation to which the directive applies is set forth. The directive is not a remedy for this condition or situation. The latter is simply the occasion for the directive. The situations envisioned are usually stated in specific terms.

In the apodosis the directive itself is given. The verb may be in the perfect, imperfect, or imperative. When the perfect and imperative are used the directive applies to single, unrepeated actions or situations. The imperfect is used in directives which apply to situations in which more than one specific action or occurrence is anticipated. In such cases the directive is limited by the conditions set forth in the protasis. It does not have general applicability to any additional future situations.

The conditional particle employed is, in nearly every case, 'im. The variation in address from singular to plural is clearly dictated by the circumstances of the speaking, whether to an individual or to a group. In no case is the singular employed when a group is being addressed. In regard to the subject matter treated in these directives, there is a wide variety with no particular subject predominating.

2. Statements of Consequences

Agreements. This particular category consists of formulations which contain terms or stipulations of agreements. The basic pattern is, "If you do thus and so, then I will do thus and so." A specific example is: "If ye will be as we are, that every male of you be circumcised, then will we give our daughters unto you, and we will take your daughters to us, and we will dwell with you, and we will become one people" (Gen. 34:15b-16). The protasis sets forth what the addressee is to do, and the apodosis sets forth what the speaker promises to do in return. A bargain is struck. There is a balance between the two sides of the agreement.

TABLE III. NARRATIVE AGREEMENTS

	Ref.	Subject	Cond.	Num.	Speaker	Adressee
Gen.	30:31	wages	'im	sg.	Jacob	Laban
	30:33	wages	'im	sg.	Jacob	Laban
	31:50	other wives	'im	sg.	Laban	Jacob
	34:15f.	seduction	'im	pl.	Jacob's sons	Hivites
	34:17	seduction	'im	pl.	Jacob's sons	Hivites
	43:4f.	Benjamin	'im	sg.	Israel's sons	Israel
Jos.	2:14	espionage	'im	pl./sg.	two spies	Rahab
	2:20	espionage	'im	sg.	two spies	Rahab
Jud.	4:8	war	'im	sg.	Barak	Deborah
	9:15f.	parable	'im	pl.	bramble	trees
	11:9f.	war	'im	pl.	Jephthah	elders
	11:30	vow	'im	sg.	Jephthah	Yahweh
	14:12f.	riddle	'im	pl.	Samson	people
ISm.	1:11	vow	'im	sg.	Hannah	Yahweh
Ruth	3:13	levirate	'im	sg.	Boaz	Ruth
Jer.	40:4b	release	'im	sg.	Nebuzaradan	Jeremiah
Zec.	11:12	wages	'im	pl.	Zechariah	Israel

The conditional particle employed is always 'im. Sometimes the agreement is restated in negative form as in the case of Jacob's wages (Gen. 30:31, negatively restated in 30:33), the seduction of Dinah (Gen. 34:15f., negatively restated in 34:17), and the espionage at Jericho (Jos. 2:14, negatively restated in 2:20).

The mutuality implied in these agreements is their most striking feature, even in the case of the vow (Jud. 11:30, I Sam. 1:11). They are unlike any of the formulations in the legal portions of the Old Testament. The case of the relationship between Jacob and Laban is instructive concerning the character of the agreement. Laban has Jacob enter into an agreement that the latter will not take wives other than the daughters of Laban nor will he mistreat them. The agreement is referred to as a covenant.[4] Quite obviously it is a covenant between equals. In return for Jacob's promise, a boundary is set up between Laban and Jacob. This story is aetiological in character and apparently explains the boundary between the Israelites east of the Jordan and the nomadic Arameans.[5] The details of the agreement possibly reflect an actual agreement between early Israelite and Aramean groups.[6]

In the agreement formulations Yahweh is never the speaker, but in two instances he is addressed as party to the agreement outlined. The first of these concerns Jephthah's vow to Yahweh (Jud. 11:30) and the second concerns Hannah's vow to Yahweh (I Sam. 1:11). There may be some question whether the vow is properly considered under the category of agreement. It does conform to the basic structure of the agreement. Something is requested and something is promised. The main difference concerns the one addressed. The striking of bargains with divinity is not extraordinary in the history of man. The bargain is usually rather onesided, however, since the role of divinity in making such agreements is a passive one and only becomes active in the fulfillment of the object of the vow.

Threats and Promises. The formulations of this variety may be further subdivided into two groups on the basis of their subject matter, whether non-religious or religious.

a. Non-religious threats and promises. The intent is usually to warn of the consequences of certain future actions or to exert pressure on future courses of action through promises which would reward the desired action. An example is Jer. 26:15 - "Only know for certain that if ye put me to death, ye will bring innocent blood upon yourselves and upon this city and its inhabitants, for in truth Yahweh sent me to you to speak all these words in your ears."

TABLE IV. NON-RELIGIOUS THREATS AND PROMISES

	Ref.	Subject	Cond.	Num.	Speaker	Addressee
ISm.	3:17	Samuel's vision	'im	sg.	Eli	Samuel
	26:19	David's flight	'im	sg.	David	Saul
IISm.	19:14	Amasa's position	'im	sg.	David	Amasa
IKg.	13:8	Jeroboam's gratitude	'im	sg.	man of God	Jeroboam
	22:28	battle	'im	sg.	Micaiah	Ahab
IIKg.	18:22f.	wager	kî/'im	pl./sg.	Rabshakeh	Hezekiah
Jer.	26:15	Jeremiah's trial	'im	pl.	Jeremiah	princes
ICh.	12:18	David's army	'im	pl.	David	recruits
IICh.	18:27	battle	'im	sg.	Micaiah	Ahab
Neh.	13:21	sabbath	'im	pl.	Nehemiah	merchants

In the protasis a future situation is envisioned in which the behavior of the addressee is at stake. Two formulations deviate slightly from this pattern, for in I Sam. 26:19 and 12:18 the protasis refers to present conditions, but they are conditions which have implications for future action. In the apodoses there are a variety of rather vague threats and promises. Only in two instances (I Kgs. 13:8 and II Kgs. 18:22f.) is the threat or promise specific. Clearly these threats and promises are designed to control future action, and in this respect are similar to the religious threats and promises.
b. Religious Threats and Promises. The formulations of this kind are similar in several respects to the threats and promises interspersed in the legal portions of the Old Testament. The intent behind the religious threats and promises is to persuade and encourage loyalty to Yahweh and observance of his commandments. An example is I Kgs. 3:14 - "And if thou wilt walk in my ways, keeping my statutes and my commandments, as thy father David walked, then I will lengthen thy days." The chief design of these exhortations is to control the addressee's future action in so far as that is possible. The will of the speaker is not directly commanded; yet it is clearly evident to the one addressed and is supported by persuasive threats and promises.

TABLE V. RELIGIOUS THREATS AND PROMISES

	Ref.	Subject	Cond.	Num.	Speaker	Addressee
Jos.	24:15	covenant renewal	'im	pl.	Joshua	Israel
	24:20	foreign gods	kî	pl.	Joshua	Israel

(Table V. cont.)

ISm.	7:3	foreign gods	'im	pl.	Samuel	Israel
	12:14f.	commandments	'im	pl.	Samuel	Israel
	12:25	wickedness	'im	pl.	Samuel	Israel
IKg.	2:4b	faithfulness	'im	sg.	Yahweh	David
	3:14	commandments	'im	sg.	Yahweh	Solomon
	6:12	commandments	'im	sg.	Yahweh	Solomon
	9:4-7	ordinances	'im	sg.	Yahweh	Solomon
	11:38	commandments	'im	sg.	Ahijah	Jeroboam
ICh.	22:13	ordinances	'im	sg.	David	Solomon
	28:9	serving Yahweh	'im	sg.	Yahweh	Solomon
IICh.	7:17f.	ordinances	'im	sg.	Yahweh	Solomon
	7:19f.	ordinances	'im	pl.	Yahweh	Israel
	15:2	seeking Yahweh	'im	pl.	Azariah	Asa/people
	30:9	return to Yahweh	'im	pl.	couriers	Israel

The protasis introduces the subject of loyalty, usually in rather general terms, using such expressions as "serve Yahweh," "return to Yahweh,"
"keep my commandments," "observe the statutes and ordinances," and "seek
him." The conditional particle preferred is 'im. In the one exception, Jos.
24:20, the subject is apostasy. The use of the particle kî may indicate the
writer's belief in the likelihood of such a thing happening.[8] The apodosis
ordinarily contains a simple promise or threat. Jos. 24:15 and I Sam. 7:3
are exceptions to this general rule. In both of these an imperative demand
is expressed in the apodosis along with the threat or promise. In all of the
religious threats and promises there is an attempt to impress the will of
Yahweh upon the addressee, but this is done indirectly, through persuasion.

There are several exhortations in I Kings which refer to "my (Yahweh's)
statutes" and "my commandments" or "my ordinances".[9] These passages reveal
considerable stylistic similarity and are most likely a product of the
Deuteronomic school. Joshua 24 and I Sam. 7 and 12 may also be deuteronomistic.

Counsels. The formulations in this category range from the advice of
a wife to a husband (I Sam. 19:11b) to the counsel of a man of God to a king
(II Ch. 25:7f.). The subjects treated all involve rather weighty matters.
The speaker is usually one having authority, but his authority is implied in
what he knows rather than in his position. The word spoken carries this
authority, but there is a question as to whether the advice will be followed.
The speaker does not directly impose his will on the addressee in that he

does not promise or threaten anything himself. Rather, he appeals to reason
in order to transfer his will to the addressee. The following is an example:
"If thou dost not save thy life tonight, tomorrow thou shalt be killed"
(I Sam. 19:11b).

TABLE VI. NARRATIVE COUNSELS

Ref.		Subject	Cond.	Num.	Speaker	Addressee
Jud.	16:13b[10]	Samson's strength	'im	sg.	Samson	Delilah
ISm.	19:11b	Saul's intrigue	'im	sg.	Michal	David
IISm.	19:8	David's mourning	'im	sg.	Joab	David
IKg.	12:6f.	Rehoboam's reign	'im	sg.	elders	Rehoboam
IIKg.	2:10	Elijah's ascension	'im	sg.	Elijah	Elisha
IICh.	10:6f.[11]	Rehoboam's reign	'im	sg.	elders	Rehoboam
	25:7f.[12]	army of Ephraim	'im	sg.	man of God	Amaziah
Est.	4:14	intercession	'im	sg.	Mordecai	Esther

The advice itself is set forth in the protasis. The latter suggests a
future action or situation involving the addressee[13] or a present action or
situation continuing in the future.[14] The conditional particle employed is
always 'im, and it is usually followed by a verb in the imperfect. The
actions or situations specified are mostly singular in nature, without antic-
ipation of general application. An example of special interest is I Kings
12:6f.

> Then King Rehoboam took counsel with the elders who had stood
> before Solomon his father while he was yet alive, saying, "How
> dost thou advise me to answer this people?" And they said to
> him, "If thou wilt be a servant to this people today and serve
> them, and answer them and speak good words to them then they
> will be thy servants forever."

The advice given by the elders applies broadly to Rehoboam's administration
and the manner in which he will treat the people. The identity of these
elders is clarified by the phrase, "who stood before Solomon his father
while he was yet alive." In other words, they were Solomon's advisers, his
wisemen.

The apodosis indicates a result which is to follow upon the course of
action described in the protasis. In most cases its effect is to strengthen
the counsel given.

If-You Formulations in Prophetic Speech

In the prophetic books there are three major kinds of speech: accounts, prayers, and prophetic speeches.[15] A number of If-You formulations occur in the prophetic speeches proper and in prophetic speeches which are preserved within accounts. The same questions may be put to this material: Who is the speaker? Who is the addressee? and What is happening in this speaking?

The first question involves the more general problem of the identity of the speaker in prophetic speech. The prophet obviously is speaking, but he claims to be speaking for Yahweh. This pattern of speech is similar to the messenger formula of the ancient Near East.[16] The prophet speaks, but it is the will of Yahweh that is being expressed, not the will of the prophet.[17]

On the basis of the second and third questions concerning the addressee and the content, only one major category emerges in the If-You formulations in prophetic speech. This category is composed of religious threats and promises. The remainder of the If-You formulations compose a heterogenous collection of formulations, some of which have already been encountered in the narrative material.

1. Statements of Consequences

Threats and Promises. As in the case of the religious threats and promises in narrative, the intent behind the prophetic exhortations is to persuade and encourage loyalty to Yahweh and observance of his commandments. An example is Isa. 1:19f., "If you are willing and obedient, ye shall eat the good of the land; but if ye refuse and rebel, ye shall be devoured by the sword; for the mouth of Yahweh has spoken." The design of these exhortations is to control the addressee's future action in so far as that is possible. In other words, there is an attempt to impress the will of the speaker upon the addressee by means of threats and promises.

TABLE VII. PROPHETIC THREATS AND PROMISES

Ref.	Subject	Cond.	Num.	Addressee	Apodosis
Isa. 1:19f.	obedience	'im	pl.	Israel	promise/threat
7:9b	war	'im	pl.	royal house	threat

(Table VII. cont.)

	58:9b-10	service	'im	sg.	Israel	promise
	58:13f.	sabbath	,im	sg.	Israel	promise
Jer.	4:1f.	return	'im	sg.	Israel	instruc./ promise
	7:5-7	social justice	'im	pl.	Judah	promise
	13:17	refusal to listen	'im	pl.	Israel	threat
	13:22	Israel's suffering	kî	sg.	Israel	threat
	17:24	sabbath	'im	pl.	Judah	promise
	17:27	sabbath	'im	pl.	Judah	threat
	22:4f.	social justice	'im	pl.	royal house	promise/ threat
	26:4-6	heed prophets	'im	pl.	Judah	threat
	33:20	restoration	'im	pl.	Israel	promise
	42:10	flight to Egypt	'im	pl.	remnant	promise
	42:13-15	remaining in the land	'im	pl.	remnant	threat
Zec.	3:7	loyalty	'im	sg.	Joshua	promise
Mal.	2:2	glory to Yahweh	'im	pl.	priests	threat

The protasis introduces the subject of loyalty frequently in more specific terms than those in narrative material or in legal material. Matters such as sabbath observance,[18] social justice,[19] and flight to Egypt[20] come into play. In addition to these specific matters, one also finds vague generalizations such as obedience,[21] refusal to listen,[22] and return to Yahweh.[23] The conditional particle most commonly employed is 'im. There is one exception, Jer. 13:22, in which kî is employed, probably to express the likelihood of such a situation arising, in this case the question of Israel's suffering.

The one addressed in these threats and promises can be the nation collectively, a particular group within the nation, or an individual. In the great majority of cases the nation is addressed, sometimes by the religio-national title Israel, sometimes by the narrower designation, Judah. Three groups addressed are the royal house,[24] the remnant left from the fall of Jerusalem,[25] and the priests.[26] Only one formulation contains an address to an individual, in this case to Joshua the High Priest.[27]

The apodosis contains either a promise or a threat.[28] This criterion is an indicator of the context in which the exhortations occur. Those in which the apodosis contains a promise occur as part of an oracle of judgment. In either case, it is clear that the formulation does not stand alone but in some way is part of the oracular statement. What then is its relative position in the oracle? and, beyond that, what is its function? Westermann has quite correctly indicated that the exhortation and warning are not to be considered as independent prophetic speech types,[29] but as secondary elaborations of primitive oracular forms.[30] By this it is not meant that they are editorial; rather, they are secondary in the sense that they develop from the original oracular statements. The threats and promises in If-You style are part of more extensive exhortations.

It is necessary to take note of the distribution of the If-You styled prophetic exhortations in determining how they came to be part of prophetic speech. By far the largest number of such formulations occur in the Book of Jeremiah and most of these within prose contexts. Only two religious threats and promises in If-You style occur in the prophetic material pre-dating Jeremiah, Isa. 1:19f. and 7:9b, and only four in the material postdating Jeremiah, Isa. 58:9b-10, 58:13f., Zec. 3:7, and Mal. 2:2. Their marked usage in Jeremiah poses the question of their authenticity. Are they part of the genuine words of the prophet or do they stem from some other source? They have usually been considered deuteronomic in origin.[31] To this question we must return in the following analysis and to the more general question whether exhortations in If-You style are indigenous prophetic modes of expression.[32]

2. _Miscellaneous_ _Formulations_. There remain in the prophetic material a number of If-You formulations of varied kinds which deserve some mention. In the Book of Isaiah there is but one If-You styled formulation which does not fit the category of exhortation. In the Book of Jeremiah there are five formulations, several of which are not unlike the varieties noted in narrative context. Three formulations of the promise-threat variety occur in Ezekiel. A series of rhetorical questions occurs in Zech. 7:5f. In the following table these formulations are outlined.

TABLE VIII. MISCELLANEOUS PROPHETIC FORMULATIONS

Ref.	Subject	Cond.	Num.	Speaker	Addressee
Isa. 21:12	morning/night	'im	pl.	watchman	people

(Table VIII. cont.)

Jer.	12:5	endurance	kî	sg.	Yahweh	Jeremiah
	15:2	Judah's destruction	kî	sg.	Yahweh	Jeremiah
	15:19	return	'im	sg.	Yahweh	Jeremiah
	38:17f.	siege of Jerusalem	'im	sg.	Jeremiah	Zedekiah
	49:9	Edom	'im	sg.	Yahweh	Edom
Ezk.	3:19	responsibility	kî	sg.	Yahweh	Ezekiel
	3:21	responsibility	kî	sg.	Yahweh	Ezekiel
	33:8f.	responsibility	kî	sg.	Yahweh	Ezekiel
Zec.	7:5f.	fasting	kî	pl.	Yahweh	people/ priests

Isa. 21:12 contains a quotation from the city night watchman in If-You style which the prophet has incorporated into his oracle. This is a unique example and has no clear counterpart in any of the materials treated thus far. Two of the formulations in Jeremiah occur in conjunction with laments of the prophet, 12:5 and 15:19. In chapter 12 the prophet takes up a theme commonly treated in wisdom, the suffering of the righteous. The complaint is followed by a divine reply in vv. 5ff. In v. 5 two rhetorical questions, the first in If-You style, are quoted, indicating even more demanding times for the prophet.[33] Such observations on life are commonly employed in wisdom. The rhetorical question as a speech pattern differs from other If-You formulations discussed in that the will of the speaker is not directly involved. Rather he is simply making a dispassionate observation of "the way things are," in this case, by means of the rhetorical question. In Zech. 7:5f. there are two rhetorical questions in If-You style. Following Jeremiah's lament in 15:15-18 is another divine reply in If-You style (v. 19), in this case a promise. In the three remaining examples there is a directive (15:2), a counsel (38:17f.), and a rhetorical question (49:9). All three of the If-You formulations in Ezekiel (3:19, 3:21, 33:8f.) pertain to the prophet's responsibility as outlined by the divine word. They have the character of promise and threat.

If-You Formulations in Wisdom

The wisdom literature of the Old Testament falls within three broad categories: 1) short units including the popular proverb and the sentence, 2) medium units including riddles, parables, fables, allegories, and wisdom

poems, and 3) large units consisting of extended reflective essays. If-You
formulations occur in both the first and third categories. In Job, Proverbs,
and Ecclesiastes the words spoken are the words of the wiseman, and he
speaks on the authority of his own knowledge. Only in Job, however, is the
speaker specifically identified.[34]

The great majority of the If-You formulations in wisdom fall within the
scope of the directive or the counsels. The remainder fall into a small
group of rhetorical questions.

1. Conditional Demands

Directive. The wisdom directive is another speech pattern which has a
counterpart in the narrative If-You formulations. The range of speakers and
addressees is, however, not so broad. The speaker is always the wiseman.
This is the case even in the Joban speeches in which the speaker is named.
Job, his friends, and the mysterious Elihu all speak as wisemen. In the Book
of Proverbs the address form is always the non-specific "my son." This is
the customary address in ancient Near Eastern wisdom literature.[35] The custom probably issues from the fact that the primary responsibility for the
instruction of sons resided with the father.[36] In like fashion the wisdom
teacher stood in a paternal relationship to his pupils.[37]

The wisdom directive is of a more general character than the narrative
directive. The latter usually anticipates specific situations, while the
former applies its word to broader categories of experience. The situations
are not once-and-for-all but are subject to repetition. An example of the
wisdom directive is: "My son, if sinners entice thee, consent thou not"
(Prov. 1:10).

TABLE IX. WISDOM DIRECTIVES

	Ref.	Subject	Cond.	Num.	Speaker	Addressee
Prv.	1:10	temptation	'im	sg.	sage	my son
	3:30	contention	'im	sg.	sage	my son
	6:1-5	surety for neighbor	'im	sg.	sage	my son
	23:1-3	eating with a ruler	'im	sg.	sage	unspecified
	25:21f.	enemy	'im	sg.	sage	unspecified
	30:32f.	idle talk	'im	sg.	sage	unspecified
Job	11:14	iniquity	'im	sg.	Zophar	Job

40

(Table IX. cont.)

	Ref.	Subject	Cond.	Num.	Speaker	Addressee
	33:5	disputation	'im	sg.	Elihu	Job
	33:32f.	disputation	'im	sg.	Elihu	Job
	34:16	disputation	'im	sg.	Elihu	Job, etc.
Ecc.	5:7-9	justice	'im	sg.	Qoheleth	unspecified

The protasis sets forth the condition or situation, while the apodosis contains the directive itself. The relationship between the parts of the sentence is a relationship of general situation and action appropriate thereunto. In the narrative directive the relationship is one of specific situation and action appropriate thereunto. In the wisdom directive a rule is outlined which is to be considered valid in all future situations of the variety described in the protasis. In the narrative directive a rule is outlined which is designed for only one specific situation.

2. Statements of Consequences

Counsels. The counsel in wisdom literature is not unlike that in narrative context. The same qualifications apply here as in the case of the directive. The wisdom counsel is of a more general character than the narrative counsel. The latter usually anticipates specific situations, while the former is applied to broader categories of experience. An example of the counsel is:

> My son, if thou receive my words
>   and treasure up my commandments with thee,
> making thine ear attentive to wisdom
>   and inclining thine heart to understanding;
> yes, if thou criest out for insight
>   and raise thy voice for understanding,
> if thou seek it like silver
>   and search for it as for hidden treasures;
> then thou shalt understand the fear of Yahweh
>   and find the knowledge of God. Prov. 2:1-5

TABLE X. WISDOM COUNSELS

	Ref.	Subject	Cond.	Num.	Speaker	Addressee
Prv.	2:1-5	receiving wisdom	'im	sg.	sage	my son
	3:24	rewards of wisdom	'im	sg.	sage	my son
	9:12	being wise	'im	sg.	wisdom's maids	unspecified
	22:17f.	words of the wise	kî	sg.	sage	unspecified
	24:13f.	finding wisdom	'im	sg.	sage	my son
Job	8:4-6	divine justice	'im	sg.	Bildad	Job
	11:13	repentance	'im	sg.	Zophar	Job

(Table X. cont.)

Prv.	13:10	partiality	'im	pl.	Job	friends
	19:18f.	child discipline	'im	sg.	sage	unspecified
	23:13f.	child discipline	kî	sg.	sage	unspecified
	23:15f.	wise heart	'im	sg.	sage	my son
Job	22:23-26	return to God	,im	sg.	Eliphaz	Job

The formal structure of the counsel is the same as that in narrative context. In the protasis the advice itself is given. It points to a future action or situation which applies to the addressee, usually in terms of appropriating wisdom. The admonition is of a general nature, not advice for one specific case, but advice which may be applied broadly to the life of the addressee.

In the apodosis there is described a consequence of the course of action outlined in the protasis. It is designed to strengthen the counsel with the prospect of reward. The reward is also set forth in rather general terms such as: "thou shalt understand the fear of Yahweh," (Prov. 2:5) "thou wilt not be afraid," (Prov. 3:24) and "it will be pleasant" (Prov. 22:18).

Rhetorical questions. There is one small group of formulations which remain. The rhetorical question is a kind of counsel put interrogatively, as in Job 35:6 - "If thou hast sinned, what dost thou accomplish against him?" It is easily restated as a counsel in the following manner: "If thou hast sinned, thou dost accomplish nothing against him."

TABLE XI. WISDOM RHETORICAL QUESTIONS

	Ref.	Subject	Cond.	Num.	Speaker	Addressee
Prv.	22:26ff.	pledges	'im	sg.	sage	unspecified
	24:12	adversity	kî	sg.	sage	unspecified
Job	34:6f.	sin	'im	sg.	Elihu	Job

In the rhetorical questions the protasis outlines the situation which is the occasion for the question. The question itself is stated in the apodosis. The exhortative character of the rhetorical question is fairly obvious. While it sets forth a question, the answer is already implied

therein. By raising a question, the answer to which is obvious, the rhetorical question is intended to persuade and convince. It is a less direct
method of persuasion than the straightforward counsel. The counsel gives
directly what the rhetorical question only implies.

Summary

The foregoing analysis of the formal structure of the If-You formulations in the non-legal Old Testament material has revealed five clearly
defined speech patterns in If-You style which may be divided on the basis of
the presence of the imperative, either grammatical or intended: 1) Conditional Demands - a) requests and b) directives; 2) Statements of Consequences - a) agreements, b) threats and promises, and c) counsels. The If-
You formulations are primarily linguistic devices for expressing the will of
the speaker. The five varieties noted represent a broad spectrum for the
accomplishment of this central purpose. The request and the directive stand
at opposite ends of the spectrum. The request is a word spoken by a subordinate to a superior. Its appeal is to the good nature and benevolence of
the latter. The agreement is a word usually spoken between equals and
appeals to the mutuality of the relationship. Threats and promises are words
spoken by an authority to an equal or to a subordinate. Its appeal is to
the persuasive power of fear and hope. The counsel is a word spoken by an
authority to a subordinate. Its appeal is to the reasonableness of that
which is set forth. The directive is also the word of an authority to a
subordinate but its appeal is to the authoritativeness of the speaker's
position. These relationships are graphically set forth in the following
table.

TABLE XII.   COMPARISON OF CATEGORIES

Category	Speaker	Addressee	Appeal
Request	subordinate	superior	benevolence
Agreement	equal	equal	mutuality
Threat/Promise	authority	equal/subordinate	fear/hope

(Table XII. cont.)			
Counsel	authority	subordinate	reason
Directive	authority	subordinate	authority

If-You formulations in prophetic speech for the most part are threats and promises and most of these appear in the Book of Jeremiah, a fact to which we must return. In wisdom the instruction and the directive predominate. They are both more general in content than their narrative counterparts.

Concerning the singular-plural variation there are some noteworthy tendencies. In the narrative If-You formulations only the instructions reveal a marked preference for either singular or plural, namely the singular. In the other narrative categories neither singular nor plural predominate. In the wisdom If-You formulations the singular is preferred, with only one exception (Job 13:10). In the prophetic threats and promises there is some preference for the plural address form. In those cases in which the singular is employed in prophecy, the address is frequently to the nation as a collective unit.

III. IF-YOU FORMULATIONS IN OLD TESTAMENT
LEGAL MATERIAL

The If-You formulations appear to combine characteristics of the

standard casuistic (If) formula on the one hand and characteristics of the

commands and prohibitions (You-Shall) on the other. With casuistic law they

share the hypothetical form of a protasis introduced by kî or ʾim which sets

forth a certain condition under which or to which the law applies. They

differ from casuistic laws in that they generally employ the second person

singular or plural for their verbs rather than the third person. With the

commands and prohibitions they share the direct address style.

A closer examination of the If-You formulations further reveals dif-

ferences and variations within this group itself. A most obvious variation

is the use of the singular in some and the plural in others. The singular-

plural variation, notably in the Book of Deuteronomy, has occasioned consid-

erable scholarly debate. The variation has been employed as a means of

isolating an Urdeuteronomium. As early as 1891 C. H. Cornill used this cri-

terion, believing certain laws to be secondary because of their formulation

in the plural.[1] Shortly thereafter in 1894, both K. Steuernagel and W.

Staerk published works on Deuteronomy based on the changing forms of address[2].

The early discussion of this criterion tended to see it as a result of the

combination of two separate editions of the Book of Deuteronomy (one in the

singular, the other in the plural[3]) or as a combination of three separate

editions (one in the singular, two in the plural[4]). The theory was largely

based on the recognition of two introductory speeches (Deut. 1-4 and 5-11).

The theory of separate independent editions has met with little acceptance.

More convincing are the completion hypotheses, as by Horst, Hospers and von

Rad[5], which explain the variation in address on the basis of successive

editorial supplements. Most recently, G. Minette de Tilesse[6] and Henri

Cazelles[7] have presented arguments for solving the problem by assigning the

singular sections to the primitive text and the plural sections to the
Deuteronomistic History, as the latter has been analyzed by M. Noth.[8] The
best solution appears to be to regard the original text of Deuteronomy as
having been formulated in the singular. A subsequent editorial process has
added short comments and edited the text, sometimes replacing singular passages with ones in the plural. Very few laws in Deuteronomy are presently
formulated in the plural.

In the other legal portions of the Old Testament the situation concerning singular and plural usage is quite different. Whereas in Deuteronomy
a law formulated in the singular would seem to belong to the original text,
elsewhere, for example in the Holiness Code, this would not necessarily be
the case. One needs to investigate, however, the question whether the
singular-plural variation reflects different life situations.

Another means of differentiation, already employed in the analysis of
the comparative material, is the presence or absence of the imperative. On
this basis the If-You formulations in the Old Testament legal material may be
divided into two categories. Those formulations with the imperative constitute much the larger category which is more easily handled if divided
according to subject matter. Accordingly, they may be treated under four
headings: humanitarian, ceremonial, holy war, and juridical.

A. The Humanitarian If-You Formulation

The prescriptions of this type are not laws in the strictly juridical
sense, for they do not describe a case subject to legal action (what is), nor
do they prescribe penalties (what shall be). The humanitarian If-You formulations differ from casuistic law in that they express a formal obligation or
prohibition incumbent upon the one whose situation is described in the
protasis and do not provide remedies in the form of penalties. Like the
commands and prohibitions, they anticipate little, if any, disobedience. A
typical example of this type of formulation is Exod. 23:4 - "If thou meet
the ox of thy enemy or his ass going astray, thou shalt bring it back to
him."

The protasis normally begins with k $\hat{i}$, although ,im is employed in at least three instances (Exod. 22:24, 22:25, and Deut. 22:2). It envisions a situation which may be an action of the addressee or a situation in which the addressee is involved. In the former case, a second person imperfect form of the verb follows immediately upon the opening k $\hat{i}$ (or ,im). In the latter case, the third person imperfect form of a verb is employed (with the exception of Deut. 22:2). The conditions described in the protasis have to do with situations of distress. In all of the humanitarian If-You formulations the second person appears already in the protasis.

In the apodosis a moral responsibility is placed upon the individual. It is cast in the preceptive style[9] of the commands and prohibitions. The verb is in the second person imperfect, MacKenzie's "preceptive imperfect".[10] Sometimes it is preceded by the negative l $\bar{o}$. The apodosis contains a divine instruction pertaining to the situation described in the protasis. The demand placed upon the individual is sometimes supported by a motive clause (Exod. 22:25f., Lev. 19:33f., Dt. 15:12-15, 22:8, 24:10-13, 24:19). These moral formulations, then, insist upon ethical and religious values of a markedly humanitarian outlook and are designed to evoke sympathy for those in dire circumstances.

The following information concerning the humanitarian formulations is given in the table: literary stratum, subject treated, conditional particle employed, and the singular-plural variation.[11] For the sake of comparison, You-Shall formulations with a similar content are also included. In the table, the latter are indicated by the absence of a conditional particle.

TABLE XIII.   HUMANITARIAN FORMULATIONS

Ref.		Stratum	Subject	Cond.	Num.
	I.		Treatment of Oppressed		
Ex.	21:2-6	BC	slaves (Hebrew)	k $\hat{i}$	sg.
	22:20	BC	sojourner		sg.
	22:21-23	BC	widow and orphan		sg.
	22:25	BC	poor (loans)	,im	sg.
	22:26f.	BC	poor (pledge)	,im	sg.
	23:6	BC	poor (justice)		sg.
	23:9	BC	sojourner		sg.

(Table XIII. cont.)

				kî	sg./pl.
Dt.	15:1-6	D	poor (debts)		sg.
	15:7-10	D	poor (loans)	kî	sg.
	15:12-15	D	slaves (manumission)	kî	sg.
	15:16f.	D	slaves (permanent)	kî	sg.
	23:16f.	D	slaves (runaway)		sg.
	24:6	D	poor (pledge)		sg.
	24:10-13	D	poor (pledge)	kî	sg.
	24:14f.	D	hired servant (poor)		sg.
	24:17f.	D	sojourner, etc.		sg.
	24:19	D	sojourner, etc.	kî	sg.
	24:20	D	sojourner, etc.	kî	sg.
	24:21	D	sojourner, etc.	kî	sg.
Lv.	19:9f.	HC	poor and sojourner		sg.
	19:14	HC	deaf and blind		sg.
	19:33f.	HC	sojourner	kî	sg./pl.
	23:22	HC	poor and sojourner		sg.
	25:25	HC	poor (property)	kî	sg.
	25:35-37	HC	poor (care for)	kî	sg.
	25:39-40	HC	poor (hired servant)	kî	sg.
	25:47-49	HC	poor (redeeming)	kî	sg.
		II.	Treatment of Peers		
Ex.	23:1	BC	false witness		sg.
	23:2f.	BC	perversion of justice		sg.
	23:4	BC	enemy's livestock	kî	sg.
	23:7	BC	false charge		sg.
	23:8	BC	bribes		sg.
Dt.	16:19f.	D	perversion of justice		sg.
	19:14	D	removal of landmarks		sg.
	22:1	D	stray livestock		sg.
	22:2	D	stray livestock	'im kî	sg.
	22:8	D	parapets		sg.
	23:20f.	D	interest on loans		sg.
	23:25	D	neighbor's vineyard	kî	sg.
	23:26	D	neighbor's grain	kî	sg.
	25:1-3	D	punishment limited	kî	sg.
Lv.	19:13	HC	neighbor/servant		sg.
	19:15	HC	injustice		pl./sg.
	25:14	HC	buying and selling	kî	sg./pl.
		III.	Treatment of Animals		
Ex.	23:5	BC	livestock in distress	kî	sg.
Dt.	22:4	D	livestock in distress		sg.
	22:6f.	D	mother bird	kî	sg.
	25:4	D	muzzling of ox		sg.

The humanitarian If-You formulations may be divided into three classes
on the basis of the subject which is protected by the injunction: I. the
oppressed classes, those people who had neither a strong family nor adequate
finances for their security (the poor, the slave, the sojourner, the widow,
and the orphan); II. one's own peers, those with whom one might have every-
day exchange; III. animals which are at a disadvantage due to circumstances.

It is immediately apparent that this style of formulation is found in
all three major bodies of law in the Old Testament. It is found already in

the Book of the Covenant. There it comprises part of a small group of humanitarian legislation, the remainder of which is cast in preceptive style without "if", namely, 22:21, 22:22-24, 23:1, 23:2f., 23:6, 23:7, 23:8, 23:9. Of the If-You formulations, two are devoted to the institution of lending (22:25, 22:26f.), two to responsibility for an enemy's livestock (23:4 and 23:5). There is also the law pertaining to Hebrew slaves (Ex. 21:2-6). It has been argued that this particular ordinance did not employ the second person address but rather was cast in third person form.[12] The entire section concerning slaves (21:1-11) is thoroughly casuistic in form. It is on this basis and on the manner in which the law concerning the female slave is introduced (v. 7) that this conclusion has been drawn. There can be very little doubt that the original was cast in the impersonal form of the casuistic law. There remains the possibility, however, that the present form of v.2 is based on a similar law which had an If-You form. The fact that both Lev. 25:39f. and Deut. 15:12-15, which contain similar admonitions, are cast in second person form argues strongly for such a conclusion.

Certain formulas are found appended to a portion of these humanitarian laws. The first of these is a recollection of the sojourn in Egypt: "Thou shalt not wrong a stranger or oppress him, for ye were strangers in the land of Egypt" (Exod. 22:21). A second formula warns of Yahweh's reaction should he hear the cry for help of one who has been afflicted: "If thou do afflict them, and they cry out to me, I will surely hear their cry" (Exod. 22:23). Also following the prescription against keeping a garment in pledge overnight, there is the injunction: "And if he cries to me, I will hear, for I am compassionate" (22:27b). Such motive clauses apparently reinforce prescriptions which would be difficult to enforce through penalties.[13] Humanitarian motives in the Book of the Covenant also appear in conjunction with certain of the old ritual laws. To the sabbatical cycle prescription (23:10) is appended the phrase "that the poor of thy people may eat, and what they leave the wild beasts may eat" (23:10b). Again, there is appended to the Sabbath law (23:12) the phrase, "that thine ox and thine ass may have rest, and the son of thy bondmaid, and the stranger, may be refreshed" (23:12b).

The largest number of humanitarian If-You formulations are found in the Deuteronomic legislation which goes far beyond the Book of the Covenant in its tendency toward humanitarian concerns. The humanitarian legislation of Deuteronomy does not occur in any one distinct form. The forms vary again between You-Shall and If-You style, with an approximately equal number of each. The subjects covered by these humanitarian laws reveal little tendency toward a correlation between subject matter and the two styles, with the exception that most procedural matters, such as injustice and bribery, are cast in You-Shall style. There are laws concerning the sojourner in both You-Shall and If-You styles. The same is true for laws concerning slaves, widows and orphans, and lending. Of the If-You formulations, two are devoted to the poor (15:7-10, 24:10-13), two to slaves (15:12-15, 15:16f.), three to the sojourner, the widow and the orphan (24:19, 24:20, 24:21), four to responsibility towards one's neighbor and brother (22:2, 22:8, 23:25, 23:26) and one to animals (22:6f.).

Certain motive formulas also frequently accompany humanitarian legislation in Deuteronomy, both in the If-You and in the You-Shall formulations. They may be grouped under four headings: 1) the blessing of land and material advances, 2) reminiscence of the Egypt event, 3) a rather general type which mentions the Divinity in some connection and 4) the "cry" of the oppressed to Yahweh. Among the humanitarian laws of the Deuteronomic Code the blessing occurs three times. It is appended to the law concerning release from indebtedness: "For Yahweh thy God will bless thee in all thy work and in all that thou dost undertake" (15:10b). The law concerning manumission of slaves every seventh year is followed by the phrase, "So the Lord thy God will bless thee in all that thou doest" (15:18). And to the law regarding interest on loans there is appended, "that the Lord thy God may bless thee in all that thou dost undertake in the land which thou art entering to take possession of it" (23:20). The logic of these appendages is apparent: blessing is appended to rather uneconomic injunctions.

Another frequent appendage is the mention of the land granted by Yahweh. In one case it occurs in connection with the blessing, this following the prescription mentioned above concerning usury. Again in connection with the perversion of justice there is the injunction: "Justice, and only justice, thou shalt follow that thou mayest live and inherit the land which Yahweh thy God gives thee" (16:20). The promised land is also mentioned in relation to the removal of landmarks (19:14) and in relation to the exposure of one who had been hanged (21:23). Along with the themes of blessing and land there is frequent recital of the "Egypt" event. For example, in Deut. 24:17f., following the injunction concerning justice for the sojourner, the widow, and the orphan, is the admonition, "but thou shalt remember thou wast a slave in Egypt and Yahweh thy God redeemed thee from there; therefore, I command thee to do this" (24:18). The same admonition is appended to the law of gleaning (24:19-22), and to the law of manumission (15:12-18).

The fourth appendage to be considered is the warning lest one who is oppressed should cry unto Yahweh. This formula occurs only once in the humanitarian legislation of the Deuteronomic Code in the prescription concerning the hired servant: "lest he cry against thee to Yahweh, and it be sin in thee" (24:15b). Significantly, all of the motive clauses discussed are religious in nature and all have reference to divinity in some measure.

It may be said that within the humanitarian legislation as a whole there is a bias toward the oppressed classes, a bias which is also found in the prophetic literature and in the "wisdom" of the Old Testament and the ancient Near East. Furthermore, the same bias is evident in the kingship ideology of the ancient Near East. In the Deuteronomic material there is a new emphasis upon the value of life, both human and animal. The laws are not simply prescriptions for proper social relations. By contrast, they display a preponderance toward the finer points of morality. The most unusual instance of this trend is the prescription regarding the building of parapets around the roof of a house (22:8) in order to protect human life. Such a law indicates a definite sensitivity regarding a person's responsibility for the well-being of others. While it may be argued that the sensitivity involved is to the guilt which might be incurred should someone fall from a

man's roof and die, it is more likely that the warning against blood guilt is
an afterthought given to strengthen the law.

According to the analysis of von Rad concerning the Deuteronomic material, the words of exhortation, of warning and promise, are of a secondary
nature. It is parenetic material, that is, hortatory material developed by
the priests to drive home to the hearer the full impact of the law. In von
Rad's words, "it is law preached".[14] That such a conclusion is unnecessary
will be shown in the following analysis.

A large number of the humanitarian laws of the Deuteronomic legislation
have no parallel anywhere in the Torah. In addition, even those laws which
do have parallels are characterized in Deuteronomy by an even greater humanitarian appeal. For example, the law concerning the garment taken in pledge
in Exod. 22:25-27 provides that the garment shall not be kept overnight, so
that the poor man may have it to cover himself while he sleeps. In Deut.
24:10-13, there is an additional prohibition which admonishes one who has
made a loan not to go into the debtor's house to fetch his pledge but to
stand outside while it is brought to him. An expansion of the slave laws
found in Exod. 21:2-11 occurs in Deut. 15:12-18; the slave that is set free
is to be given enough cattle, grain and wine to help him enter into an
independent state, and release applies to a female slave as well as to a
male.

The humanitarian If-You formulations of Deuteronomy do not all occur
closely together, yet there is some tendency toward grouping. The first
three of these (Deut. 15:7-10, 15:12-15, 15:16f.) are found within the context of stipulations of a generally clement nature (Deut. 15:1-18), having to
do with persons sold into bondage and with the year of release from indebtedness. These two separate, but related, matters have undoubtedly been
brought together by the Deuteronomic editor. Chapter 24 of Deuteronomy contains an almost unbroken series of humanitarian If-You formulations concerning
the sojourner, the widow, and the orphan. These were the dispossessed classes
with no strong clan to stand for their rights. Normally in the ancient Near
East their protection was a particular responsibility of the king. In the

form in which the injunctions occur here they are addressed to the individual.
The remainder of the humanitarian If-You formulations in Deuteronomy occur
among various laws apparently without any conscious arrangement.

Outside the Book of the Covenant and Deuteronomic legislation, six
occurences of the humanitarian If-You form are in the Holiness Code. The
humanitarian legislation of the Holiness Code is not as extensive as that of
Deuteronomy. There are only four humanitarian laws in You-Shall style (Lev.
19:9f., 19:13, 19:14, 19:15). Of the If-You formulations, one deals with the
sojourner (19:33f.), one with buying and selling (25:14) and the remainder
concern the poor (25:25, 25:35-37, 25:39-40, 25:47-49). Ordinarily, the
plural does not occur in the humanitarian regulations. Two prescriptions in
the Holiness Code (19:33f. and 25:14), however, are exceptions to this rule.

In the case of Lev. 19:33f. there is a problematic mixture of singular
and plural usage: "If a stranger sojourn with thee in your land, ye shall
do him no harm. The stranger that sojourneth with you shall be unto you as
the home-born among you, and thou shalt love him as thyself; for ye were
strangers in the land of Egypt: I am the Lord your God." These two verses
are not organically tied to their context. They appear with a series of
ethical stipulations which are rather loosely connected. A reconstruction of
the original nucleus might appear thus: "If a stranger sojourn with thee,
thou shalt do him no harm." This original nucleus formulated in the singular has been elaborated by the addition of a prescription in the plural[15]
further describing how the sojourner is to be treated, that is, as the home-
born, as expressed pregnantly in the singular form: "thou shalt love him as
thyself." A motive clause has also been supplied.

Lev. 25:14 may likewise have had an originally singular form. As it
stands, it presents a rather curious mixture of singular and plural and is,
as Noth has indicated, "phrased in a very defective manner and doubtless with
secondary enlargements."[16] A reconstruction of the original might look as
follows: "If thou sell anything unto thy neighbors, or buy of thy neighbor's
hand, thou shalt not wrong one another." The remainder of the humanitarian
If-You formulations in the Holiness Code compose a series of ordinances con-

cerning the impoverished brother in Lev. 25. All four of these regulations
contain the conditional clause, "If thy brother becomes poor" (vv. 25, 35,
39, 47). They are connected in their present context with the release of the
year of jubilee as set forth in the first part of the chapter. They belong to
the realm of family law and may not, therefore, have originated in connection
with the year of jubilee which is probably a relatively late invention and
which may never have actually been put into effect. The impoverished-brother
laws are probably rationalizations of ancient practice. They belong to the
same kinship ethos as does blood vengence. This is apparent in the usage of
the word gōēl which means not only "redeemer" but also "nearest of kin", as
in Ruth 2:20, and appears in the phrase gōēl haddām, usually translated
"avenger of blood". The "avenger of blood" and the "redeemer" of the impoverished brother are one and the same. The fact that these impoverished-
brother laws are designed for a settled agricultural society, suggests that
they may be an early adaptation of the ancient kinship ethos to the conditions of settled life. It is quite possible that they are based on an
originally independent series of redemption regulations.[17]

These humanitarian prescriptions, because they carry no penalty except
divine displeasure, are not laws that could be enforced and administered by
the civil authority. On the contrary, the authority behind all of these prescriptions is that of the invisible Yahweh as in the case of the commands and
prohibitions.

In most cases the If-You humanitarian formulations are closely associated with laws set forth in You-Shall style. The use of the second person
already in the protasis is suggestive of such a close relationship. In
addition, a law in If-You style may be extended by a You-Shall styled formulation as in Deut. 15:7-10a -

> If there is among you a poor man, one of thy brethren,
> in any of thy towns within thy land which the Lord thy
> God gives thee, thou shalt not harden thy heart or shut
> thy hand against thy poor brother. But thou shalt open
> thy hand to him, and lend him sufficient for his need,
> whatever it may be . . . Thou shalt give to him freely,
> and thine heart shall not be grudging when thou givest
> to him.

Here the apodosis of the main sentence is extended by two additional You-
Shall formulations. This, and the similarity of subject matter covered by the
humanitarian You-Shall and If-You formulations, strongly suggests that the
latter are not to be thought of as separate independent forms, but rather as
a variation and extension of the You-Shall form. In the following analysis
it will be shown that You-Shall and If-You styles occur together elsewhere
(e.g., in Egyptian and Hittite materials.)[18] Furthermore, no relation to the
so-called casuistic (If) law is apparent.

The question of ultimate origin is more difficult. Related to it is
the question of the origin of the humanitarian spirit of this legislation,
particularly that of Deuteronomy. A widespread assumption has been that the
Deuteronomic legislation was influenced primarily by the prophets of the
eighth century.[19] Moshe Weinfeld has argued convincingly against such a conclusion, for he believes the humanitarian concern is related to the wisdom of
the ancient Near East.[20] MacKenzie likewise has chosen to look for the
origin of this concern elsewhere, namely in the Book of the Covenant.[21]

It is quite true that humanitarian values are to be found in other
spheres. The prophets were also highly concerned about 1) the oppression of
the lower classes, particularly the poor, 2) the practice of injustice in
legal matters, and 3) the practice of dishonesty in economic dealings. Therefore Isaiah remonstrates:

> Learn to do well; seek judgment, relieve the oppressed,
> judge the fatherless, plead for the widow (Isa. 1:17).

Amos also accuses: "They hate him who reproves in the gate, and they abhor
him who speaks the truth" (5:10). In negative terms it is found in Isaiah's
derision of the Assyrian boast (Isa. 10:13-14a). Jeremiah and Ezekiel likewise reflect humanitarian values in their admonitions, e.g., Jer. 22:3,
Ezek. 18:5ff.

That the "wise men" were concerned about humanitarian social ideals
is evident from the many admonitions concerning the lower classes, removal of
landmarks, and simple justice. For example, in Prov. 19:17 there is the
sentence: "He who is kind to the poor lends to the Lord, and he will repay

him for his deed." Concerning justice, "A worthless witness mocks at justice, and the mouth of the wicked devours iniquity" (Prov. 19:28). Prov. 22:28 is an admonition against the removal of landmarks: "Remove not the ancient landmark which your fathers have set."

What is the relationship between the humanitarian moral content of the prescriptions and the If-You style? First, the If-You style is well suited to persuasion. It is the style frequently employed by the authors of ancient Near Eastern didactic literature,[22] the purpose of which is to persuade and instruct. Second, the If-You style exhibits a flavor of reasoning even in setting forth a demand. Reason is implicit to some extent in the process of applying demands critically to specific situations and conditions. The If-You style seems particularly well suited for humanitarian laws which require a maximum of persuasion.

B. THE CEREMONIAL IF-YOU FORMULATION

The ceremonial If-You formulations are so named because they have to do with the formal religious acts of the Israelite community. As in the case of the humanitarian formulations, the prescriptions of this type are not laws in the strictly juridical sense, for they do not describe a case subject to legal action nor do they prescribe penalties. They are instructions for the regulation of various aspects of cultic life, and it is the religious authority behind them which gives them force.

An example of the ceremonial If-You formulation is Exod. 20:25 - "And if thou make me an altar of stone, thou shalt not build it of hewn stones; for if thou wield thy tool upon it thou hast profaned it." This example in the Book of Exodus is part of the law of the altar (20:24-26) which in turn has been incorporated into the preface to the Book of the Covenant.

The following information concerning the ceremonial If-You formulations is given in the table: literary stratum, subject matter treated, conditional particle employed, and the singular-plural variation.

TABLE XIV. CEREMONIAL FORMULATIONS

	Ref.	Stratum	Subject	Cond.	Num.
Ex.	12:25-27	D	passover	kî	pl.
	13:5	D	unleavened bread	kî	sg.
	13:11-14	D	first-born	kî	sg.
	20:25	BC	altar construction	'im	sg.
	34:20	D	first-born	'im	sg.
Lv.	2:4	P	meal-offering	kî	sg.
	2:5	P	meal-offering	'im	sg.
	2:7	P	meal-offering	'im	sg.
	2:14	P	meal-offering	'im	sg.
	11:39	P	uncleanness	kî	pl.
	19:5	HC	peace offering	kî	pl.
	19:23	HC	fruit trees	kî	pl.
	22:29f.	HC	thank offering	kî	pl.
	23:10	HC	first-fruits	kî	pl.
	25:20ff.	HC	sabbatical year	kî	pl.
Num.	9:14	P	sojourner's offering	kî	pl.
	15:2-10	P	offerings	kî	sg.
	15:14	P	sojourner's offering	kî	pl.
	15:22-24	P	hidden sin	kî	pl.
	18:26	P	the tithe	kî	pl.
Dt.	6:20	D	credo	kî	sg.
	12:21	D	sacrifice	kî	sg.
	14:24	D	the tithe	kî	sg.
	18:6-8	D	Levites	kî	sg.
	18:21	D	false prophets	kî	sg.
	26:1	D	first-fruits	kî	sg.
	26:12-15	D	the tithe	kî	sg.

The protasis usually begins with kî although there are several cases in which 'im is employed. In all cases the second person appears already in the protasis, which defines the particular ceremonial occasion or action in which the addressee may be involved. In the apodosis an instruction is given which indicates the proper action or activity for the occasion specified.

There are five instances of formulations of this type in the Book of Exodus, two of which are similar to each other (Exod. 13:13 and 34:20). Exod. 13:13 is part of the regulations concerning the firstborn and is apparently based on the old ritual decalogue.[23] Exod. 34:20 is nearly identical in wording. The dedication of the first-born was doubtless an ancient Canaanite custom taken over by the Israelites with certain modification.[24] The regulation concerning the first-born of an ass (13:13, 34:20) was necessitated by the fact that the ass was primarily a "working" beast not ordinarily used for food, therefore not used as a sacrificial animal.[25] Thus it had to be "redeemed" or removed from profane use by breaking its neck, since

58

it could not be sacrificed. The law as it now stands is probably the result of a deuteronomic redactional process. There is no clear evidence concerning the original status of the two sections in which it occurs.[26]

Exod. 12:25-27, concerning passover, and Exod. 13:5, concerning unleavened bread, are prefaced with a formula regarding entry into the land, for example: "And when ye come to the land which Yahweh will give you, as he has promised . . . " (Exod. 12:25). Both of these have usually been regarded as part of a deuteronomic redactional process.

The law of the altar (20:24-26) has been generally regarded as a very ancient law, since it envisions rather simple conditions.[27] Immediately preceding the If-You style law concerning altars built of stone (v.25) there is a prescription in You-Shall style pertaining to the building of altars of earth. There are indications that in an earlier period natural rocks in situ were used as altars.[28] The law of the altar clearly indicates constructed altars. Since altars are unknown among other Semitic nomads,[29] it is most likely that the altar law is a product of the transition of the Israelites to settled life. The narrative in Deut. 27:5-7 reflects the custom of building altars from unhewn stones as does also Jos. 8:30f. The latter adds, "as it is written in the Book of the Law of Moses". The only Israelite altar brought to light by excavation is one from Arad dating from the 10th century B.C.[30] It is constructed of unhewn stone according to the law. It appears that the altars of the first Temple violated the law,[31] whereas those of the second and third temples were built strictly according to it.[32] There appears to be no reason for doubting the antiquity of the law. But why the prohibition against working the stone? The most likely theory concerns the primitive belief that such holy objects were spirit endowed or divinely created.[33] Using tools upon them either offended the spirit or perhaps drove it away.

The law of the altar is cast in singular address form. There seems no reason to doubt that this is its original form. The context in which it occurs employs a plural address form.

By far the largest number of ceremonial If-You formulations occur in the Book of Leviticus. Most of these have to do with offerings, the protasis pointing to the specific offering, the apodosis giving instructions for the preparation of the offering.

Lev. 2 contains a section of regulations for the preparation of the minhā or meal-offering.[34] This chapter is a complex mixture of several layers of tradition, witnessed by variations in style and address. Within it there occur no less than four instructions in If-You form (2:4, 5, 7, and 14). Vv 2b, 3, 9 and 16 contain directions for the priest; everything else concerns that which the individual worshipper needed to know in preparing his meal-offering.

Lev. 2 differs from surrounding chapters by its use, in large part, of second person form. Vv. 4, 5, 7, 8a, 13 and 14 use second person singular address, vv. 11f. use second person plural. Some commentators have regarded the second person style as a secondary intrusion. Rendtorff looks upon Lev. 2 as a conflation of the third person ritual form and the second person plural priestly tôrāh form of Begrich.[35] Klaus Koch sees the second person as the result of an editorial process, since vv. 4-7 do not seem to fit the terse, pregnant style of the priestly tôrāh form as Begrich described it.[36] Karl Elliger, however, rejects the thesis of Rendtorff concerning the existence of a ritual form behind Lev. 1-5.[37] Elliger does regard the second person usage in Lev. 2 as a later intrusion.

The problem of the appearance of the second person address in Lev. 2 is not satisfied by the analysis of Koch or Rendtorff or Elliger. If one assumes that the third person address of the context (Lev. 1-5) is primary, then one might be inclined to consider any interruption as editorial creation or editorial insertion. Such an assumption may, however, be misleading. Elliger's analysis raises serious questions concerning the existence of a ritual form as outlined by Rendtorff. The content indicates that these regulations were at least in part addressed to the laity whose task it was to prepare the meal offering. They may have originated in a practice of oral recitation by the priests to worshippers at the sanctuary.

If the second person usage is editorial, why has the editor departed here from his usual plural usage? In other cases in the editorial structure in which a second person address is employed, the plural is preferred.[38] It is more likely that the editor has simply recorded the material the way he found it. The fact that vv. 11 and 12, which are in the plural form and interrupt this second person singular address, is further evidence that the editor has not changed the form of address in this section.

If indeed the second person singular belongs to the original formulation, then Lev. 2 may well preserve a more primitive form of instruction than is found in Lev. 1, 3-5. The second person singular address would issue quite naturally from a situation in which the priests were giving oral instructions to the laity concerning the preparation of offerings. Since the minḥā required greater participation on the part of the worshipper, it may have been necessary for the priests to give more individual instruction for this particular offering.

Similar to the prescriptions of Lev. 2 are those in Num. 15:5-10 which concern various offerings. For the most part this section has a second person singular address. The contents are directions to the laity giving information necessary for the preparation of their offerings. The presence of the second person singular address here is further evidence for the original status of the second person singular address in Lev. 2.

The remainder of the If-You prescriptions in Leviticus employ the plural. In 11:39 there is a prescription concerning contact with the carcass of a dead animal, clearly a matter of clean and unclean. The first ceremonial If-You prescription in the Holiness Code is in 19:5 and treats the peace offering. The prescription immediately following in 19:9 is also in If-You style; however, the following prescriptions in this section are in You-Shall style: 19:11, 13, 15, 17, 19, 26, 29, 31, 32, and 35. The remainder of the ceremonial If-You formulations in the Holiness Code also are closely associated with formulations in You-Shall style. Other subjects treated in If-You style are the cultivation of fruit trees (19:23), a matter of ritual purity, the thank offering (22:29f.) and the offering of first fruits (23:10). The latter is prefaced by a somewhat vague formula which sets a condition of entry into Canaan: "When ye come into the land which I give you . . . ." This formula is most likely from the hand of the priestly editor. One might wish to exclude this prescription as not being an original If-You construction since the conditional and the second person appear in a somewhat vague, appended formula. On the other hand, the original form of this prescription must be considered before judging the issue. In the first place, the entry into Canaan formula does not make up the entire protasis. It actually appears to have been added as another provision to an already existing conditional. But what form would that conditional have taken in the original state? We may only conjecture at this point, but it seems likely that the original would have followed the usual priestly instruction form, employing the second person address. The original may then have appeared as follows: "When ye reap the harvest, ye shall bring the sheaf of the first fruits of your harvest to the priest." There are three other instances of such an entry formula (14:34f, 25:2 and Num. 15:2). Lev. 14:34f. is part of a section dealing with leprosy. It is cast in the form of divine speech to Moses and Aaron, most likely the work of the priestly editor. Lev. 25:2 is part of the preface to sabbath regulations, again, divine speech to Moses. This, too, appears to be the product of a redactor. In 14:34 there are additional conditional formulations, none of which is needed to preserve the sense of the prescription which follows in v. 35. In 25:2, 2b easily stands alone: "the land shall keep a sabbath unto Yahweh."

The last of the If-You formulations in the Holiness Code, 25:20ff., pertains to the sabbatical year. It is in the form of a question about a specific cultic practice.

Five ceremonial If-You formulations occur in the Book of Numbers within the context of material usually attributed to the priestly writers. The first of these is Num. 9:14, a regulation concerning the sojourner's offering formulated with plural address. One practice for both native and sojourner is required. Three other If-You styled regulations occur in Num. 15, a general section pertaining to offerings (15:2-10), another regulation concerning the

sojourner's offering (15:14) and the regulation concerning hidden sin
(15:22-24). The first (15:2-10) uses singular address, and the others (15:14
and 15:22-24) employ plural forms of address. In 15:14 the sojourner is required when he offers a sacrifice to follow the established custom. 15:22-24
is apparently based on the practice reflected in Lev. 4:2ff., which gives
detailed prescriptions for offerings to expiate hidden sin. Num. 15:24 reveals its secondary character by requiring the offering to be made "according
to the ordinance".

There is one If-You formulation in Num. 18:26, which differs in the
pattern of address. The ceremonial If-You formulations are ordinarily
addressed either to the individual or to the community in general. The prescription in Num. 18:26 - "Moreover thou shalt say to the Levites, 'When ye
take from the people of Israel the tithe which I have given you from them for
your inheritance, then ye shall present an offering from it to Yahweh, a
tithe of the tithe.'" - is the only instance in which this type of formulation
is addressed to a special group (in this case, to the Levites), and here it
comes within the context of the sections dealing with the responsibilities of,
and regulations for, the Aaronic priests and other Levites, Num. 18:1-32.

The Book of Deuteronomy contains a number of ceremonial If-You formulations. The first of these, 6:20, introduces the creed which a father is to
recite to his son. The creed itself is a recounting of the sacred history of
the Israelites. The interest here appears to be aetiological. The formula,
"when your son asks you in time to come", is simply a device employed to
introduce cultic information.

Four of the ceremonial If-You formulations in the Book of Deuteronomy
(12:21, 14:24, 18:6-8, and 26:12-15) are most likely motivated by the demand
for cultic centralization. Deut. 12:21 is part of a section which deals with
the eating of flesh, formulated largely in You-Shall style. Ordinarily only
wild game was not eaten sacrificially. With centralization it was necessary
to make allowances in the case of the eating of sacrificial animals from the
herd or flock. If the distance to the central sanctuary were too far, the
worshipper could kill and eat meat without the sacrificial rites. In

14:22-29 the practice of tithing is revamped in the light of the changed conditions brought about through centralization. This section is opened by the
command, "Thou shalt surely tithe all the yield of thy seed, which comes
forth from the field year by year" (14:22). The verb is strengthened by the
infinitive absolute. It is to "the place which he (Yahweh) will choose, to
make his name dwell there" that the tithe is to be brought. In the special
case in which it would impose a hardship on the worshipper to bring the tithe
a long distance, the regulation has been modified so that he may sell his
tithe for a price with which he may then purchase the necessary items for the
sacrificial feast at the sanctuary. Also an If-You formulation opens the
series of instructions concerning the tithe in 26:12-15. We have here the
necessary counterpart to the regulation of the tithe in 14:24. Here it is a
matter of the tithe which is not brought to the central sanctuary but given
to the local Levites, the stranger, the widow, and the orphan. This again
was necessitated by the centralization of the cult. The last regulation related to the centralization program in 18:6-8 is another provision directed
toward the Levites. In this case it is provided that the Levite shall have
access to the central sanctuary where he may come and "minister in the name
of Yahweh his God" (8:7). The exact nature of this ministry is not clear.
The term employed, $\Pi\,\daleth\,\mathcal{U}$, refers to any kind of service above menial tasks.
It is clear that these prescriptions related to centralization are the works
of those circles which produced the deuteronomic version of the law. They
were created, therefore, relatively late in the period of the monarchy.

Of the two remaining ceremonial If-You formulations in Deuteronomy, the
first (18:21) occurs in the regulation concerning false prophets (18:20f.),
and is set forth in the form of a question. The second, 26:1, has as its
subject the offering of first-fruits. Here the prescription is prefaced with
a formula similar to that in Exod. 12:25 and Exod. 13:5 which refers to entry
into the promised land.

It is clear from this survey that ceremonial If-You formulations are not
all of a kind. There are prescriptions cast in plural form (Exod. 12:25-27,
Lev. 11:39, 19:5, 19:23, 22:29f., 23:10, 25:20ff., Num. 9:14, 15:14, 15:22-24,

18:26), all of which occur in P material except Ex. 12:25-27. Prescriptions employing singular address occur in Deuteronomic strata (Exod. 13:5, 13:11-14, 34:20, Deut. 6:20, 12:21, 14:24, 18:6-8, 18:21, 26:1, 26:12-15), in P material pertaining to the meal offering (Lev. 2:4, 5, 7, 14; Num. 15:2-10), and BC (Exod. 20:25). The centralization program is reflected in four deuteronomic If-You styled prescriptions (Deut. 12:21, 14:24, 18:6-8, 26:12-15). There is one clear-cut instruction to cult personnel (Num. 18:26), in this case, the Levites. As could be expected, those prescriptions in P and HC deal mostly with matters of a specific nature while those in D are more general in their subject matter.

The prescriptions in Lev. 2 which reflect a second person singular style and the similar prescriptions in Num. 15:2-10 constitute a special case. The former appear closely related to the prescriptions of Lev. 1, 3-5, yet they stand apart from them because of their second person address. The second person here and in Num. 15:2-10 may reflect a priestly recitation of these formulations to the laity, instructing the latter in the proper preparation of the meal-offering. This raises some question whether Begrich was correct in including only plural forms in priestly tôrāh.

It is evident that many ceremonial If-You formulations are closely associated with You-Shall styled prescriptions. This association has been noted in every stratum.

C. The Holy War If-You Formulation

There is a group of laws concerning warfare which are peculiar to the deuteronomic legislation. Gerhard von Rad has argued that behind these regulations lie pre-monarchial amphictyonic traditions.[39] These old traditions of the tribal confederacy have been revived for some new situation. The identity of those who did the reviving and the situation they addressed are less certain.

The Israelite conception of holy war stems from the assumption that "Yahweh is a man of war" (Exod. 15:3). Thus, a holy war is Yahweh's war. The sacral character of its original conception is readily apparent in its main features:[40]

1. Blowing of the <u>shophar</u> (Judg. 3:27, 6:34f., I. Sam. 13:3).
2. Sanctification of the Warriors (Josh, 3:5, I Sam. 21:6, II Sam. 11:11).
3. Consultation of Yahweh (Judg. 7:9-14, 20:27f., I Sam. 28:6, I Kings 22:5) accompanied by the cultic verdict, "Yahweh has delivered . . . into your hand." (Judg. 7:15, Josh. 6:2, 8:1).
4. Exhortation not to fear (Josh. 8:1, 10:8, Judg. 7:3).
5. Transfer of Ark and holy vessels into field (Num. 31:6, II Sam. 11:11, I Sam. 14:15).
6. Confusion and panic sent by Yahweh (Josh. 10:10, Judg. 4:15, I Sam. 14:15).
7. The Ban (Josh. 7:18f., 6:17ff., I Sam. 15:3).

The deuteronomic legislation concerning holy war covers a variety of subjects, most of which are cast in If-You style. The following table contains the deuteronomic prescriptions for holy war, including those in other styles.

TABLE XV. HOLY-WAR FORMULATIONS

Ref.	Subject	Cond.	Num.	Style
7:1	foreign nations	kî	sg.	If-You
7:17	fear of the enemy	kî	sg.	If-You
20:1	fear of the enemy	kî	sg.	If-You
20:2-4	priests oration	kî	pl.	If-You
20:5-9	deferment	mî	sg.	What-Man
20:10f.	besieging a city	kî	sg.	If-You
20:12-14	besieging a city	ʾim	sg.	If-You
20:19f.	trees	kî	sg.	If-You
21:10-13	women captives	kî	sg.	If-You
21:14	women captives	ʾim	sg.	If-You
23:10-12	cleanliness	kî	sg.	If-You
23:13-15	cleanliness	---	sg.	You-Shall
24:5	newly married	kî	sg.	If

The protasis, which usually has an initial <u>kî</u>, sets forth a circumstance or situation having to do with war. In the apodosis there is given an instruction containing the proper action for the situation which has been described, and it is set forth in the preceptive style of the plain You-Shall formula.[41]

Two holy-war If-You formulations occur in chapter 7. The first (7:1) introduces a lengthy section warning against any alliance or association with foreign nations. The second is set forth mostly in You-Shall style. The second (7:17) introduces a prescription against fear of the enemy.

Chapter 20, which is devoted to the holy war in its entirety, is a complex section showing several layers of tradition. There are a number of If-You formulations within this context, the first of which introduces the war speeches (20:1). It is a general admonition against fear in the face of the enemy cast in the singular. It is not a law as such but has more the quality of paranesis. It stands apart stylistically from the speeches that follow and simply repeats in general terms that which the priests say to the people (vv. 3f.) For this reason we must assign it to the editorial framework. It is followed by the speech of the priest (vv. 3f.) in which the address changes to the plural.[42] This priestly speech calls for courage, i.e. do not fear, the victory is yours. That the priests had a function in the carrying forth of holy-war is incontrovertible.[43] They went into the field with the sacred objects, and they inquired of Yahweh concerning the outcome of battle. It is upon this latter tradition that the speech in 20:2-4 is probably based. The present form of the speech shows signs of editorial handling. Von Rad considers the plural usage indicative of its secondary character.[44] A more important consideration is the manner in which the priest's function is treated. Whereas in the original conception of holy war the priest had very definite sacral responsibilities, the transfer of the ark and the sacred vessels, the enquiry of Yahweh (perhaps by sacred lot), no mention of these are made in the deuteronomic legislation. Here the priest simply addresses the soldiers in order to give encouragement. Furthermore, it is the priest who speaks, not Yahweh as in sacral context.[45]

There follows in vv. 5-8 an interrogation delivered by the "officers" (ṣoṭerim)[46] concerning deferments. These minor royal officials were probably responsible for the registration of the soldiers and would have been the proper authorities to grant deferments. In this section, there are four cases cited which would occasion a deferment, the building of a new house which was yet undedicated (v. 5), the planting of a vineyard the fruit of which had not been brought into non-sacral usage (v. 6),[47] the case of betrothal in which the marriage had not been consumated (v. 7), and the case of faint-heartedness which would be contagious and demoralizing (v. 8). The first

three of these allowances may be based on old magical conceptions which held
that anyone who had something important to inaugurate was particularly vul-
nerable to demons.[48] Their presence in the ranks would be detrimental to
the success of the campaign, as would also that of those who were fearful.
The antiquity of deferment tradition is revealed by its mention in the legend
of Gilgamesh. Gilgamesh, who is collecting a band of men to help him cut
down the cedars of the Land of the Living and fight off the demons who
guarded them, speaks to them thus:

> "Who has a house, to his house! Who
> has a mother, to his mother!
> Let single males who would do as I
> (do), fifty, stand at my side."[49]

The sacral bases upon which the regulations in Deuteronomy stand are considerably deemphasized, if not altogether eliminated in their deuteronomic
version. The rationale which pervades them here is humanitarian. The usual
form (What-Man) of the deferment regulations, already commented upon by
Krause,[50] most likely preserves the form of the regulations as they were
originally promulgated. On the basis of other holy-war regulations which
have been redrafted for the deuteronomic legislation, any thorough editorial
revision of the deferment regulations most likely would have cast them in
If-You style.[51] The conditional and impersonal character of the What-Man
formulation is more suited to a situation in which "officers" speak to an
assembly of troops. The directness of the If-You style is more authoritarian
than such a situation would allow.

Following the "officer's" interrogation there are three laws regarding
sieges, 20:10f., 20:12-14, and 20:19f., all in If-You style. The conditions
envisioned by these prescriptions could hardly have been current before the
period of the monarchy.[52] In the accounts of the Israelite conquest of
Canaan there is no indication that siege tactics were employed. Entrance
was usually gained by means of subterfuge. The siege of a fortified city
was a more common occurrence during the period of the monarchy when the
Israelite kings began to employ the tactics of their more sophisticated
neighbors.[53] It does not seem likely, therefore, that the laws regarding

siege warfare date back to the early amphictyonic period but are more likely
a product of the period of the monarchy. In v. 14 the spoils of war are
allocated to the warriors. This is in marked contrast to the tradition recorded in Num. 31:50-54 which requires that the spoils be dedicated to Yahweh.
No such dedication is mentioned in the deuteronomic legislation, a further
indication of desacralization of older traditions.

The law against cutting down fruit-bearing trees, 20:19f., is an additional indication that these regulations are later than the amphictyonic
period, for it envisages a rather complicated type of siege-work, requiring
timber in its construction. The message of Elisha preserved in II Kings
3:16-19 (cf. also v. 25) does not reveal an acquaintance with any such law,
for, as he says, "every good tree" was to be felled. The practice of destroy-
ing an enemy's trees is known among several ancient peoples. In some cases it
seems simply a matter of destruction to wreak havoc upon the enemy.[54] Otherwise the destruction of trees probably came as a result of the need to build
war machines in the vicinity of the besieged city. To the prescription in
20:19f. there is appended a motive clause: "For is the tree of the field man,
that it should be besieged by thee?"[55]

Two holy-war If-You forms occur in the regulation regarding women captives (21:10-14) which is set within the context of other family laws. It has
a stylistic uniformity with no apparent breaks which would denote the work of
an editor. It is introduced by the same formula as in 20:1 and for this
reason should be attributed to the same deuteronomic hand.[56] While the law
has no exact parallel in the other ancient Near Eastern law codes, there does
seem to be a related custom at Mari as revealed in the royal archives.[57] The
deuteronomic law is decidely humanitarian in tone, bringing the protection of
the law even to the woman who has been taken captive. She may not be abused.
Since the law envisions the taking of such captives, it is apparently addressed
to a situation of conflict with non-Canaanite nations which would not have
fallen under the "ban".

Two If-You formulations occur in the law of the camp (23:10-15) and are
in substance doubtless more ancient than the other holy-war If-You formu-

lations. They are part and parcel of an ancient cultic mentality which regarded the ceremonial purity of the camp as of great importance to insure the
presence of Yahweh among his people.[58] The camp was a sacred place since
Yahweh himself dwelt within it. It must be kept holy. In this context, however, the interest is more weighted toward cleanliness than toward sacral
purity, which is introduced almost as an afterthought in v. 15.

The regulation regarding the newly married (24:5) repeats the substance
of 20:7. It adds the provision that the deferment is to last one year. It is
cast in conditional style, but employs the third person as in the standard
casuistic laws.

It is clear that the deuteronomic holy-war regulations, while they rest
upon old traditions, are nevertheless peculiar to the deuteronomic legislation
and represent one of the most characteristic themes of the entire book. These
laws have been modified according to the deuteronomic concept of holy war,
which is characterized by a marked desacralization. Would such a program of
desacralization likely be the creation of priests? There is good reason for
doubt since the interests of the priesthood would have tended toward the
sacral aspects of holy-war. Some clue as to the origin of these prescriptions
may be offered by the inclusion among them of the deferment regulations in
"What man" style. Such military regulations were most likely associated with
the monarchy. The king, as chief of the military, was the primary authority
in military matters. This was certainly the case among Israel's neighbors,[59]
and it is reasonable to assume that Israel in this respect would not be different. This, with the fact that the regulations point to conditions which
were not present until the period of the monarchy suggest a strong possibility
that the holy-war regulations were revised and new ones created by personnel
closely associated with the royal court.

D. The Juridical If-You Formulations

The prescriptions of this type are similar to the standard casuistic
formulations in that they set forth in the protasis a situation subject to
legal action and a penalty or remedy for that situation in the apodosis. The

following is an example of this type of formulation: "But if a man willfully
attacks another to kill him treacherously, thou shalt take him from my altar,
that he may die" (Exod. 21:14). It must be assumed that the second person
address here refers to officials, for it was they who had primary responsibility for carrying out the penalty.[60] Their identity poses a problem to
which we will return in the following discussion.

The protasis usually begins with kî and sets forth in the third person
either a case subject to legal action or a matter of judicial procedure. The
second person may be introduced, however, in a qualifying phrase such as that
in Deut. 21:22f. - "And if a man has committed a crime punishable by death,
and thou hang him on a tree, his body shall not remain all night upon the tree,
but thou shalt bury him the same day, for a hanged man is accursed by God;
thou shalt not defile thy land which Yahweh thy God gives thee for an inheritance." In the table which follows, these cases are indicated by the
letter "A". Those in which the second person does not occur in the protasis
are indicated by "B". The situations described in the protasis have to do
with criminal offences and matters which pertain to the work of the judiciary.
Only in the case of the latter does the protasis describe a case in which the
officials themselves are directly involved (Deut. 17:8-13, 21:22f.). In the
majority of cases the second person address does not appear until the apodosis,
in contrast to the If-You formulations in other categories. This fact under-
scores the peculiar character of the juridical If-You formulations. The
apodosis describes a remedy for the situation, usually in the form of penalties, which the judicial officials are to mete out. One instruction to
these officials is set forth in You-Shall style (Deut. 16:18-20).

TABLE XVI.   JURIDICAL FORMULATIONS

	Ref.	Stratum	Subject	Cond.	Num.	2nd. p.
Ex.	21:14	BC	murder	kî	sg.	B
	21:23-26	BC	miscarriage	ʾim	sg.	B
Dt.	13:2-6	D	false prophet	kî	sg./pl.	A
	13:7-12	D	apostacy	kî	sg.	A
	13:13-16	D	apostate city	kî	sg.	A
	16:18-20	D	justice	--	sg.	-
	17:2-7	D	apostacy	kî	sg.	A
	17:8-13	D	judgment	kî	sg.	B

(Table XVI. cont.)

19:1-6	D	cities of refuge	kî	sg.	A
19:8-10	D	cities of refuge	ʾim/kî	sg.	A
19:16-21	D	witnesses	kî	pl.	B
21:1-9	D	unsolved murder	kî	pl.	A
21:22f.	D	executed	kî	sg.	B
22:22	D	adultery	kî	sg.	B
22:23-27	D	rape	kî	sg.	B
25:11f.	D	indecent assault	kî	sg.	B

These forms are found only in the Book of the Covenant and in Deuteronomy. The two cases in which such a form occurs in the Book of the Covenant (Exod. 21:14, 21:23f.) appear to be additions to earlier laws. Exod. 21:12-17 contains a series of laws which require the death penalty. The characteristic expression for this occurs in the predicate standing at the end of the sentence, taking the form, môt yûmāt, "shall be put to death". These injunctions begin with a participle which describes the condemned action. Exod. 21:14 is clearly an addition to these terse formulations and may have been inserted after the initial collection of the Book of the Covenant.[61] Exod. 21:23f. is appended to the law concerning injury done to a pregnant woman. The entire section, Exod. 21:18-36, is a series of laws concerning bodily injury. They are cast in the standard casuistic style for the most part. The section has been enlarged in Exod. 21:23f. by the introduction of the lex talionis and this in an unusual style. The protasis begins with a conditional reminiscent of the casuistic formulations; however, the apodosis employs a second person singular imperfect form of the verb which is more akin to the You-Shall style of the Preceptive formulations.[62] In both of these cases, the formal responsibility for the exactment of punishment lies with the officials. The identity of these officials is not clear. In the remainder of the juridical If-You formulations, all of which occur in Deuteronomy, it is often possible to determine whether the officials addressed are elders or judges.

The remainder of the laws in this group cover a variety of subjects. In Deut. 13 there is a series of prescriptions concerning apostasy, which, according to Israelite mentality, posed a threat to the entire community. It is in this respect that it becomes a matter for juridical concern. The

seriousness of the offence is indicated by the severity of the penalty, which
in all cases is death. These prescriptions also reveal the particularly
strong deuteronomic opposition to foreign gods. The first two prescriptions
deal with false prophets (2-6) and other enticers to apostasy (7-12). As
they stand, both of these prescriptions appear to be addressed to the community in general. The regulation concerning false prophets has been expanded by an editor, who inserted the parenetic section in vv. 4b-5. These
verses are particularly marked by their use of the second person plural
address. To this law is appended the characteristic Deuteronomic formula:
"Thou shalt purge the evil from the midst of thee." (13:6). This formula is
frequently appended to laws which concern criminal offences.[63] The second
section concerning other enticers to apostasy (vv. 7-12) is obviously intended for the community at large. In v. 10 the witnesses are addressed as
the ones who must cast the first stones.[64]

The third prescription concerns the apostate city, certainly the most
difficult case and one which required special treatment. The investigation
envisioned in v. 15 seems to indicate some kind of official inquiry. The
officials to whom the law is addressed could be none other than state authorities, for only they would have the power and authority to carry out the
destruction of such an apostate city. In this regulation the holy-war ideology also comes into play. The city is to be totally destroyed and the
spoils thereof are to be put under the "ban". From this it appears that the
officials addressed had military authority as well as juridical authority.[65]

In Deut. 17 there are two juridical If-You formulations. Another prescription concerning apostasy is found in vv. 2-7. The investigation required (v. 4), and the instructions regarding witnesses (vv. 6f.) indicate
that the law is addressed to the same judiciary circles as is Deut. 13:1-16.
The second person appears already in the protasis. To this law is also
appended the formula: "Thou shalt purge the evil from the midst of thee"
(v. 7). The regulation is followed by a prescription concerning difficult
judgments which are to be appealed to the central judiciary (17:8-13). Here
the second person does not appear until the apodosis. This ordinance is

obviously a result of the deuteronomic centralization program whereby the local places of worship were closed down. The local sanctuaries had previously provided for judicial appeals. Under their jurisdiction difficult cases were solved by ordeal (Num. 5:11ff.), by oath taking (Exod. 22:7, 10) or by the casting of lots (Exod. 22:8, 28:30). The deuteronomic law provides for appeal to a central high court consisting of Levites and judges. There is widespread evidence that during the period of the monarchy the king was considered the final judge and referee in disputed cases.[66] That this was also the case at Ugarit is supported by the story of prince Yassib who challenged Keret's right to rule on the basis that the latter was no longer able to discharge his duty as supreme judge of the land.[67] Further, Daniel is referred to as a king who "is upright, sitting before the gate, beneath a mighty tree on the threshing floor, judging the cause of the widow, adjudicating the case of the fatherless."[68] Confirmation that Canaanite kings served as supreme judge comes from historical inscriptions. The Alalakh Tablets reveal that Niqmepa, a king of Alalakh during the 15th century B.C., adjudicated a case involving murder and the confiscation of property and a case concerning the extradition of fugitive slaves.[69] The Middle Assyrian laws and the Hittite laws also indicate the king's judicial function.[70] The silence of the deuteronomic law on the king's judicial function is not conclusive evidence that the king was no longer considered as the final appelate judge. Obviously, however, in a state organization such functions had to be delegated. The existence of a central judicial body is in itself evidence that the king did in fact have supreme judicial power. Only state power could establish and maintain such a body.

Chapter 19 of Deuteronomy is devoted to the juridical process. The first part of the chapter deals with cities of refuge (vv. 1-10). In this section there are two If-You formulations, 19:1 and 19:8. You-Shall styled formulations also occur (19:7 and 19:9) in the section. The cities of refuge usually have been regarded as a necessary outgrowth of the centralization program, since the outlying sanctuaries which had previously provided a place of refuge for the accidental manslayer were destroyed. Increasing knowledge of similar practices among the Phoenicians, Syrians, Greeks, and Romans suggests caution against considering the practice a Deuteronomic innovation.[71] Among many ancient Near Eastern peoples certain precincts afforded absolute security to fugitives no matter what their degree of guilt. Deuteronomy limits asylum to the accidental manslayer. The idea of asylum is also desacralized in Deuteronomy since they are no longer Levitical (i.e., temple) cities.

The ordianace in Deut. 19:16-21 concerning the malicious witness seeks to protect the judicial process itself. The basic law of witnesses is repeated in v. 15; i.e., at least two witnesses are required to convict a man. To it has been added a detailed ordinance for the adjudication of cases where perjury is suspected. The parties must come before the central judiciary ("before Yahweh, before the priests and the judges" v. 17). An investigation is required (v. 18). The lex talionis is invoked as the penalty if the witness is found guilty. The characteristic deuteronomic formula is appended: "Thou shalt purge the evil from the midst of thee." (v. 19).

The prescription in Deut. 21:1-9 concerning unsolved murder is apparently built upon an ancient ceremony. If a man is found murdered in the fields and there is no evidence regarding his murderer, the responsibility for the disposition of the matter rests upon the elders of the nearest town. If such a deed were allowed to go unexpurgated, the whole community would bear the burden of blood guilt and could become involved in blood feud. The elders of the nearest city are to come forth and bring an unworked heifer to an uncultivated valley with a running stream. There they are to break the heifer's neck, wash their hands over the heifer and declare in an oath their innocence and lack of involvement in the crime. There seems little doubt that the rite described is of great antiquity. There are regulations of similar principle in the Code of Hammurabi, which requires the governor of a district to compensate the relatives of a murdered man,[72] and in the Hittite laws which places compensatory responsibility on the occupiers of territory in which a man has died or upon the closest hamlet if the land was not privately owned.[73] The details of the rite which is to be performed indicate a

settled agricultural society. It is quite possible that it is based on a
Canaanite original. That the elders were the only officials originally involved is evident from the fact that theirs is the central role. The judges
and the Levites have only been introduced in the deuteronomic version. Their
roles here are not clearly defined. The judges as officials of the state may
have served in determining which town was closest to the murder place. The
Levites, however, seem to have no actual function other than that of on-
lookers. When the obvious deuteronomic elements have been removed, the
ordinance appears as follows:

> If anyone is found slain, lying in the open country, and
> it is not known who killed him, then the elders shall come
> forth, and they shall measure the distance to the cities
> which are around him that is slain; and the elders of the
> city which is nearest to the slain man shall take a heifer
> which has never been worked and which has not pulled the
> yoke. And the elders of that city shall bring the heifer
> down to a valley with running water, which is neither
> plowed nor sown, and shall break the heifer's neck there
> in the valley. And all the elders of that city nearest
> the slain man shall wash their hands over the heifer whose
> neck was broken in the valley. And they shall answer and
> say, 'Our hands have not shed this blood, neither have
> our eyes seen it.'

While cast in impersonal style, it is hardly like the casuistic formulas.
That this was the original form is suggested by the fact that in the present
form the direct address style occurs only in the opening and closing formulas, both of which are characteristic of the deuteronomic legislation. Here
as in other cases an old custom has been revamped in the light of new conditions. No longer is the unsolved murder a matter of local interest and
concern to be adjudicated by the elders. In the deuteronomic legislation it
is a state concern. The judges and the Levites appear not fortuitously, but
deliberately as the judicial authorities of the state.[74] The elders perform
the ancient ceremony under their watchful eyes.

The law against allowing the body of an executed man to remain exposed
overnight (21:22f.) is addressed to the judges as the authorities directly
responsible for the sentencing and execution. Since they were representatives of the interests of the community, they should see to it that the body
of the executed not remain exposed for any length of time to pollute the

76

land and make it unproductive. This ordinance is based upon ancient notions
that the fertility of the land may be impaired by such an occurrence. It
obviously originated within an agricultural society. Execution was not
achieved through hanging itself.[75] After death by other means, usually
stoning, the body of the executed was exposed by hanging as a singular mark of
disgrace and was taken as a token of divine malediction (v.23).

Deut. 22:22-30 contains a group of laws governing sexual offences. The
section reveals a mixture of singular and plural usage. The first ordinance
concerns adultery with a married woman (22:22), the second, adultery with a
betrothed woman (22:23f.), the third, rape of a young betrothed woman (22:
25-27), and the fourth, a rape of an unbetrothed young woman (22:28f.). The
addressee of these ordinances is not altogether clear. The deuteronomic legislation usually indicated when the local elders have jurisdiction.[76] The
cases which come before the elders involve family matters,[77] clear-cut cases
of blood vengeance,[78] or matters in which they represented the interests of
the city.[79] In predeuteronomic times the elders may have had jurisdiction in
cases of adultery and rape. There seems no reason to doubt that this was also
the case in the deuteronomic legislation. V. 24, "Ye shall bring them both
out to the gate of that city", seems to indicate that the matter was adjudicated in the gate which was the traditional place where the elders held forth.
Of greater importance is the fact that it is the elders who are officiating
in the immediately preceding context.[80] Adultery and rape were matters of
family and local concern. For this reason and because state interests were
not directly affected, these matters were not placed under the jurisdiction
of the judges.[81]

The remaining juridical If-You prescriptions in the deuteronomic legislation concern a particular case of bodily injury (25:11f.). If a woman
interferes in a fight between her husband and an opponent by assaulting the
opponent's genitals, her hand is to be cut off. At first it may seem somewhat strange that such a case should be made into a generally valid law. A
similar ordinance occurs in the Middle Assyrian Laws.[82] The punishment required there, however, is rationalized according to the extent of the damage.

If only one testicle is injured, one of the woman's fingers is to be cut off. If both testicles were injured, the woman is to be blinded. That the penalty in the Israelite law was to be carried out by the judges is indicated by the admonition, "thine eye shall not pity" (v. 12).

The juridical If-You formulations thus treat four different types of criminal offences,[83] homicide (Exod. 21:14, Deut. 21:1-9), religious crimes (Deut. 13:2-6, 7-12, 13-16, 17:2-7), sexual offences (22:22, 22:23-27), and certain cases of assault (Exod. 21:23-26, Deut. 25:11f.). In addition to these, the deuteronomic legislation contains several ordinances designed to regulate the judicial process itself (Deut. 17:8-13; 19:1-6, 8-10, 16-21; 21:22f.). Apart from the juridical If-You formulations, criminal offences are also treated in the relative formulations and the participial formulations (including the curses). Generally, laws set forth in relative and in participial style stipulate death as penalty; otherwise, vague formulas are appended. They are characterized by a strongly religious tone and cover many of the same general subjects covered by juridical If-You formulations.[84] Their adjudication was probably in the hands of the priests.

The juridical If-You ordinances represent a stage in the history of Israelite law in which public officials are given responsibility to adjudicate criminal matters. Exod. 21:23-26[85] seems to indicate that the lex talionis, previously a private matter, is partly coming under the jurisdiction of public officials. The deuteronomic judiciary reform brought the evolution of Israelite jurisprudence one step further by establishing a central high court and state appointed judges in every city. The appearance of Levites on the high court along with secular magistrates is probably attributable to the pre-deuteronomic situation in which sacral courts served to adjudicate cases of appeal. Tradition has influenced the deuteronomic reformers at this point. In addition, the fact that religious matters were being adjudicated by the state called for the presence of religious authorities on the high court.

The juridical If-You formulations are dissimilar to the more common casuistic laws in function as well as in form. The use of the second person derives from the situation out of which these ordinances emerged, that is, one in which rules and regulations governing the juridical process were spoken directly to those most responsible for it. The appearance of more general admonitions concerning justice, likewise in the second person (You-Shall), also suggests that this is the case. A series of these admonitions occurs in Deut. 16:19 - "Thou shalt not pervert justice; thou shalt not show partiality; and thou shalt not take a bribe, for a bribe blinds the eyes of the wise and subverts the cause of the righteous."[86] Israelite legislation is not alone in providing instructions to judges in such personal form. Egyptian, Assyrian, and Hittite instructions to judges are also cast in second-person address as the following analysis will show.[87]

The common casuistic laws are arbitration decisions which specify what one party is to do in particular problem "cases". In contrast, the juridical If-You formulations have to do more with the juridical process itself; many such formulations do not deal with problem "cases", but with procedural matters. They are closer to relative and participial laws in terms of the subjects they treat.

E. If-You Formulations Without the Imperative

There remain a number of formulations without the imperative which fall within the category of parenesis. They all belong to the classification of threats and promises. The protasis sets forth the situation of being obedient and of following the commands, statutes and ordinances.

In these obedience formulations there is a marked preference for the conditional particle im. This is probably based on grammatical considerations since, as previously noted, im with the imperfect normally indicates present or future possibility. Since the use of $k\hat{i}$ seems to indicate probability,[88] im is more fitting for the threats and promises. In the questions regarding cultic matters and in the entry formulations above, $k\hat{i}$ is almost exclusively employed, thus indicating the likelihood of such things happening. In matters of obedience, however, the question is left open, for the result is not at all assured. An example is Exod. 15:26, "If thou wilt diligently hearken to the voice of Yahweh thy God, and do that which is right in his eyes, and wilt give heed to his commandments and keep all his statutes, I will

put none of the diseases upon thee which I put upon the Egyptians; for I am

Yahweh thy healer." In all cases, the second person is introduced already in

the protasis.

In the apodosis there may appear one of two kinds of statements: 1) a

divine threat of impending disaster in the case of disobedience, or 2) a

divine promise of future blessedness in terms of land, protection, or pros-

perity. In the former the appeal is to fear, in the latter, to hope.

TABLE XVII. FORMULATIONS WITHOUT THE IMPERATIVE

	Ref.	Stratum	Subject	Cond.	Num.
Ex.	15:25b-26	D	heed commandments	ʾim	sg.
	19:5f.	D	keep covenant	ʾim	pl.
	23:22	D	Yahweh's angel	kî/ʾim	sg.
Lv.	26:3	HC	observe commandments	ʾim	pl.
	26:14-16	HC	observe commandments	ʾim	pl.
	26:18	HC	hearken to Yahweh	ʾim	pl.
	26:21	HC	walking contrary	ʾim	pl.
	26:23f.	HC	walking contrary	ʾim	pl.
	26:27f.	HC	walking contrary	ʾim	pl.
Dt.	4:25	D	graven image	kî	sg./pl.
	8:19	D	other gods	ʾim	sg.
	11:13	D	observe commandments	ʾim	pl.
	11:22	D	observe commandments	kî/ʾim	pl.
	28:1	D	observe commandments	ʾim	sg.
	28:13	D	observe commandments	kî	sg.
	28:15	D	observe commandments	ʾim	sg.
	28:58	D	observe law	ʾim	sg.
	30:9f.	D	observe commandments	kî	sg.

The peculiar parenetic style of Deuteronomy has long been recognized.[89]

The more recent analysis of the deuteronomic material by von Rad has further

underlined the exhortative character of that book.[90] He believes this char-

acter to have been impressed upon the book by the public rehearsal of the law

by the Levites.[91] O. Bächli attributes it to the public recitation of the law

by the king,[92] whereas E. W. Nicholson believes it to have originated with the

prophetic circles of northern Israel.[93] M. Weinfeld points to scribal circles

for the origin of this exhortative character,[94] which, as the following anal-

ysis will show, is closer to the actual ethos from which it stems.

Deuteronomy is not alone in bearing a marked parenetic quality. The

Holiness Code likewise contains legal instructions in parenetic form.[95] At

the same time, the similarities between the two bodies of law should not be
exaggerated. There is little stylistic similarity in phraseology. Furthermore, the plural form of address is preferred in the Holiness Code whereas
the singular prevails in Deuteronomy. Where the plural does occur in deuteronomic material, it is best attributed to later editing. The Holiness
Code is clearly a priestly creation which is not the case with Deuteronomy.
In the priestly sections of the Pentateuch the standard form for addressing
the community is the second person plural. This also seems to be the usual
form of the priestly tôrāh, except in those cases where the subject matter
demands the singular address.[96] From this it does not appear reasonable to
assume similar circles of origin for the Holiness Code and deuteronomic parenetic If-You formulations. Additional strength is given to this argument by
the following considerations: 1) the deuteronomic formulations frequently
strengthen the verb (imperfect) in the protasis by prefixing the participle
to it,[97] 2) the entry formula so prevalent in Deuteronomy is absent in the
Holiness Code, 3) there is a balance between threat and promise in Deuteronomy whereas in the Holiness Code the threat is more pronounced, and 4) the
Holiness Code is represented as divine speech whereas Deuteronomy is set
forth as a speech of Moses. Thus the parenetic style of Deuteronomy is suf-
ficiently different from that of the Holiness Code that we should look to
non-priestly circles for the origin of the former.[98]

Summary

In the foregoing chapter the endeavor has been to analyze the If-You
formulations which occur in the legal portions of the Torah, to differentiate
types where possible, and to relate these types to their Sitz im Leben. It
is fairly obvious that the prescriptions which are formulated in the If-You
style do not belong to a single uniform type. There are formulations which
employ the imperative and are closely related to the preceptive laws (You-
Shall). The humanitarian, ceremonial, and holy-war formulations belong to
this first group. In humanitarian legislation, an area requiring persuasion,
nearly half of the prescriptions are in If-You style. Ceremonial legislation

is cast in both singular and plural address form. It has been shown that ceremonial If-You formulations are closely related to ceremonial formulations in You-Shall style. Holy-war legislation, found exclusively in Deuteronomy, is set forth predominantly in the If-You Style.

2   The juridical If-You formulations constitute a special grouping. They exhibit some similarities to the casuistic law and to the relative and participial formulations. They represent a stage in the development of law in which the state is assuming responsibility for certain criminal matters which had previously been handled otherwise. They also are employed in the regulation of the juridical process. Their form derives from the situation of their use, i.e., as instructions to judicial officials.

3   A large number of If-You formulations fall under the category of parenesis (threats and promises) and are structurally different from laws as such. While the Holiness Code contains a number of parenetic If-You formulations, they are different from those in the deuteronomic legislation by their use of the plural.

So far, the results of this investigation reveal a deuteronomic partiality for the If-You style, nearly always in the singular. Of greater import is the fact that those interests which are most characteristic of Deuteronomy are pervaded by the If-You style. The humanitarian concern, the centralization program, and the laws for holy war are all set forth in this style. Deuteronomy also contains several threats and promises in If-You style. In addition, most of the juridical If-You formulations occur in Deuteronomy. It would be impossible to remove the If-You styled portions of Deuteronomy without doing great damage to its basic character. A close relationship between the You-Shall style and the If-You style has been suggested. This is based on the observation that in the law codes the two styles frequently occur together and treat the same subjects. The relationship is most apparent in the humanitarian legislation. The circles responsible for the creation of the Deuteronomic law found in the If-You style a useful tool in presenting their version of Israelite law.

IV. IF-YOU FORMULATIONS IN ANCIENT
NEAR EASTERN TEXTS

While the existence of If-You formulations in extrabiblical texts has
not gone unnoticed,[1] yet there has been no attempt to give them detailed
treatment. The extant ancient Near Eastern texts offer a rich body of material for comparison with Israelite literature. If-You styled formulations
occur with some regularity in the following kinds of material: didactic and
wisdom literature, vassal treaties, and instructions to various officials.
Conditional formulations with second person address occur in other contexts
such as narratives and rituals, but not with any degree of regularity. The
ritual texts are written mostly in third person style; however, a few do
employ the second person address form.[2] Conditional formulations are used to
introduce rituals or are used at the beginning of sections. The reference of
these conditionals is usually one of time, not one of cases.

Didactic and Wisdom Literature

The universality of practical wisdom in the ancient Near Eastern world
is well-attested.[3] It was expressed generally as a quality of great rulers
and counselors. Its specific expressions came to be embodied in proverbs,
instructions, and other literary forms. Associated with this kind of wisdom
was the "wise scribe" (sopher hakam) who acted as its custodian.[4] A sharp
distinction probably should not be made between the scribe and the wise man.
Both were among the educated, trained in scribal schools, and frequently employed in governmental service. In Egypt, as probably elsewhere, the scribal
office was set in a class by itself.[5]

Archaeological investigations of the last hundred years have made avail-
able for study numerous examples of the wisdom cultivated by the learned
scribes. Among these are the so-called "instructions," collections of precepts attributed to ancient kings and revered scribes. Some of these "instructions" take the form of tightly structured, succinct words of advice.
Others are longer, more complex structures, which form a unit about the size

of a paragraph. None of them reveal any obvious rhythmic qualities which
might indicate the molding of oral recitation over long periods of time. If-
You formulations are found in eight complete or nearly complete books of "instructions" from Egypt and in two fragmentarily preserved "instructions."[6]
In addition to the Egyptian "instructions," If-You formulations occur in an
Akkadian text, a fragmentarily preserved collection of Akkadian precepts and
instructions which dates prior to 700 B.C.[7] If-You formulations also occur
in the one extant wisdom composition written in Aramaic, "The Words of
Ahiqar."[8]

The questions of speaker, addressee and content also may be applied to
the didactic and wisdom literature. Three subdivisions are apparent, directive, threat and promise, and counsel. Again, these may be divided on the
basis of the presence or absence of the imperative, either grammatical or
otherwise implied.

1. Conditional Demands

Directive. By far the largest number of If-You formulations in wisdom
context falls within the category of directive. The same general observations
apply here as in the case of the Old Testament wisdom directive. Its word is
applied to broad categories of experience. An example of the wisdom directive
is: "If thou art one to whom petition is made, be calm as thou listenest to
the petitioner's speech" (Ptah-Hotep, 1.265).

TABLE XVIII. NEAR EASTERN WISDOM DIRECTIVES

	Ref.	Subject	Num.
Ptah-Hotep	85	leadership	sg.
	120	table	sg.
	149	trustworthiness	sg.
	175	economic standing	sg.
	199	son	sg.
	265	petition	sg.
	275	approaching women	sg.
	320	household and wife	sg.
	364	influence for good	sg.
	366	speech	sg.
	430	wealth	sg.
	465	relation to friend	sg.
Meri-Ka-Re	21	dangerous man	sg.
	25	dangerous man	sg.

(Table XVIII. cont.)

Hor-dedef		founding household	sg.
Ani	viii, 1	mother's example	sg.
Amen-em-opet	Ch. 13, 5	poor man's debt	sg.
	28, xxvi, 10	widow in fields	sg.
P. Insinger	23, 16	journey	sg.
	24, 11	disciplining crowd	sg.
Ka-Gemni	(Erman, p.99)	table manners	sg.
	(p. 100)	table manners	sg.
'Onchsheshonqy	6, 11	prosperity	sg.
	6, 16	keeping mind on work	sg.
	6, 19	pampering self	sg.
	6, 20	first impressions	sg.
	7, 3	servant's work	sg.
	7, 9f.	pride	sg.
	7, 17	servants	sg.
	8, 15	pampering self	sg.
	10, 8	loyalty to master	sg.
	10, 9	respect for master	sg.
	11, 9f.	appraisal of one's ability	sg.
	12, 7	willingness to intercede	sg.
	12, 22	accusations	sg.
	13, 12	wife's infidelity	sg.
	13, 13	servants	sg.
	14, 8	care in speaking	sg.
	14, 22	deceit	sg.
	15, 7	sharing wealth	sg.
	15, 18	honesty	sg.
	15, 21	responsibility	sg.
	15, 22	business sense	sg.
	16, 4	help in trouble	sg.
	16, 13	swearing falsely	sg.
	17, 5	acquiring wealth	sg.
	17, 18-20	loyalty to master	sg.
	18, 3	saving	sg.
	18, 22	keeping word	sg.
	19, 5	enemy	sg.
	19, 15-17	courage to live	sg.
	19, 19	respect for master	sg.
	19, 25	learning	sg.
	21, 23	thirst	sg.
	21, 25	journey	sg.
	22, 2	premature rejoicing	sg.
	22, 3	control over situations	sg.
	22, 18	talking to master	sg.
	24, 15	cursing master	sg.
	27, 4	hypocrisy	sg.
Eloquent peasant	150f.	doing justice	sg.
Ahiqar	ix 123-141	resourcefulness	sg.
		borrowing food	sg.
		repaying loan	sg.
	x 142-158	humility	sg.
Akkadian Counsels	K 3364 B27	keeping promise	sg.
	B28	giving encouragement	sg.

As in the Old Testament wisdom directive the protasis sets forth the condition or situation to which the directive applies. These conditions or situations are of a general nature and the directive expressed in the apodosis is to be considered valid in all future situations of the variety described.

The addressee is represented as the son of the speaker, the speaker being a scribe or other official. The directives in this class treat of the proper behavior for members of the scribal profession. Many areas of life are touched upon, ethics, diplomacy, and even table manners. But the common frame of reference, almost without exception, is relational. Problem areas pertaining to interpersonal relations are envisioned and directives applied to those situations. In some cases, it is simply a matter of how to get along with people and organize a proper household. In a few instances certain humanitarian concerns are lifted up, such as the indebtedness of the poor man:

> If thou findest a large debt against a poor man, make it into three parts, forgive two, and let one stand (Amen-em-opet, Ch. 13, 5).

There is the oft-repeated admonition concerning deference to the widow:

> Do not recognize[lit., "find"]a widow if thou catchest her in the fields, nor fail to be indulgent to her reply (Amen-em-opet, Ch. 28).

In addition there is an admonition regarding the sharing of wealth:

> When you have reached your prime and acquired much property, let your brother share your wealth ('Onchsheshonqy, 15, 7).

2. Statements of Consequences

There are a number of If-You formulations in the wise counsels which are not accompanied by the imperative, most of them falling into the category of instruction.

Counsel. The formal structure of wisdom counsel here is similar to that in the Old Testament wisdom material. The advice itself is given in the protasis with its consequence outlined in the apodosis. An example from the comparative material is:

> If thou art satisfied with false chewings, they are a pastime for thy spittle (Amen-em-opet, Ch. 23, 15).

TABLE XIX. NEAR EASTERN WISDOM COUNSELS

	Ref.	Subject	Num.
Ptah-Hotep	365	silence	sg.

(Table XIX. cont.)			
	476	hearing	sg.
Amen-em-opet	1, 15	hearing	sg.
	23, 15	table habits	sg.
'Onchsheshonqy	8, 4-6	seeking advice	sg.
	8, 9f.	imprisonment of scribe	sg.
	10, 7	care in speaking	sg.
	14, 9	doing kindness	sg.
	20, 7	taxes	sg.
	22, 16	hunger	sg.
Dispute over Suicide	55	burial	sg.
Eloquent Peasant	54-55	justice	sg.

The subjects treated in these formulations represent some of the usual interests in the didactic and wisdom literature, such as the guarding of one's speech. In contrast to the directive, the counsel deals less with relational matters. Rather, in envisioning future situations which may confront the addressee, practical observations concerning that which is appropriate or inappropriate are set forth in the protasis.

Other formulations. Three If-You formulations without the imperative belong in categories other than the counsel. There is a threat of a non-religious nature and one rhetorical question. As previously noted, the rhetorical question is a kind of exhortation put interrogatively.

TABLE XX. MISCELLANEOUS NEAR EASTERN WISDOM FORMULATIONS

Ref.	Subject	Num.
Threat		
Dispute over Suicide 49f.	delaying death	sg.
Rhetorical Question		
Eloquent Peasnat 165f.	violence	sg.

It should be noted that simple commands and prohibitions (without "if") are also found in didactic and wisdom literature. They tend to outnumber the If-You formulations which are closely associated with them. An example is:

> Do justice whilst thou endurest upon earth.
> Quiet the weeper; do not oppress the widow;
> supplant no man in the property of his father;
> and impair no official at their posts . . . (Meri-ka-re).[9]

In other places commands and prohibitions may follow upon an If-You formulation, for example:

> When thou art a young man and takest to thyself a wife and art settled in the house, set thy eye on how thy mother gave birth to thee and all (her) bringing thee up as well. Do not let her blame thee, nor may she (have to) raise her hands to the god, nor may he (have to) hear her cries (Ani).[10]

It is clear that there is considerable agreement between the If-You categories found in Old Testament material and those found in the Near Eastern material. Further there is some correspondence in proportional distribution. In both the Old Testament and in the Near Eastern material the directive constitutes the largest category and the counsel is second.

Noteworthy is the fact that the Instruction of 'Onchsheshonqy displays a preference for the If-You formulation. Glanville dates this work not later than the fifth or fourth centuries B.C.[11] If this dating is correct, we have evidence that the If-You form continued to be used in wisdom context on into the period of the late Israelite monarchy. The first five columns contain a story about 'Onchsheshonqy and the events leading up to his writing of the instruction. It is possible, according to Glanville,[12] that the instruction actually predates the narrative. 'Onchsheshonqy is identified as a priest of P-RE' who has been imprisoned for complicity in a plot against the Pharaoh. While in prison he writes the instruction for his son. The content is mainly practical advice, covering themes reminiscent of the earlier Egyptian wisdom books. Glanville believes the book shows closest affinity to Ani. The moral standard does not appear to be exceptionally high.

If-You Formulations in Regulations for Officials

Among the documents from the royal archives of the ancient Near East, there are a number of regulations[13] of the kings which are addressed to various officials. Most of the extant regulations of this nature are Hittite in origin, and come from the royal library at Hattusas. The regulations cover a variety of subjects. They are addressed to palace personnel, including kitchen workers, craftsmen, and servants,[14] and to temple officials.[15] Two Hittite

instructions to judicial officials reveal a use of second person style.[16]   In
both cases, military officials are addressed.   It is clear from these texts
that military officials performed judicial functions.   From Nuzi comes evidence indicating a similar kind of practice.[17]   There, the designation for a
judicial official was halzuḫlu which apparently indicated the officer in
charge of a fortress.[18]   Other than the Hittite regulations there is one
Sumero-Akkadian text, the so-called "Farmer's Almanac,"[19] containing directions
pertaining to the more important activities that a farmer must perform to
ensure a successful crop.   The text mentions "royal barley" (1.64-72).
Whether this is any indication that the almanac is royal in origin is open to
question.   The text closes with the acknowledgement that the regulations are
those of the god Ninurta, the son of Enlil (1.109-11).   If-You styled formulations are also employed in an Assyrian medical text which gives prescriptions for bruises and swellings and in an Egyptian text concerning the installation of the Vizier.[20]

     There is a significant difference between regulations for officials and
the didactic and wisdom tests.   In the latter, the balance of the situations
envisioned and treated are of a general nature, whereas in the former, specific
situations are envisioned and prescribed.   There are paragraph size units in
the didactic and wisdom texts as well, but there are also short, terse formulations in the latter which are not present in the regulations.

1. Conditional Demands

          Directive.   There is but one kind of formulation in regulations for
officials which is accompanied by the imperative, the directive.   While the
structure of the directive in this context is similar to that which occurs in
the didactic and wisdom texts, its content is closer to the directive in the
Old Testament narrative context.   Its word is applied to specific situations
whereas the wisdom directive concerns broader categories of experience.   An
example of the directive of the regulations is:

          Further: You who hold the plow-oxen of (the gods), if you
          sell a plow-ox, or kill it and consume it, (if) you appro-
          priate it for yourselves (while it belongs) to the god
          (saying): "It died from emaciation, or it broke (its legs),
          or it ran away, or the bull gored it" and consume it yourselves,

90

and it afterwards becomes known, you will replace the
ox. If however it does not become known, you will go
before the god. If you are acquitted, (it is due to)
your patron god; if you are convicted, it is considered
a capital sin for you. ("Instructions for Temple
Officials")[21]

TABLE XXI.   DIRECTIVES TO OFFICIALS

Ref.		Subject	Num.
Temple Officials	ii,1ff.	sacrificial food	pl.
	ii,60ff.	celebrating festivals	pl.
	iv,10ff.	planting grain	pl.
	iv,25ff.	plow-oxen of the gods	pl.
	iv,35ff.	animals for rites	pl.
	iv,56ff.	animals for rites	pl.
Military Instructions	A,I,7-9	performing service	sg.
	A,I,20f.	performing service	sg.
	A,I,26f.	misrepresenting king	sg.
Farmer's Almanac	1-12	irrigation	sg.
	22-40	plowing	sg.
	41-47	plowing	sg.
	48-63	sowing	sg.
	64-86	watering	sg.
	87-99	winnowing	sg.
	100-108	prayers	sg.
Medical Texts No.	221, 1.4	bruises or swellings	sg.
No.	224, 1.19	bruises or swellings	sg.
Rekh-mi-re	4f.	judicial procedure	sg.
	13f.	judicial procedure	sg.

As in the Old Testament directive in narrative context, the protasis
sets forth the specific condition or situation to which the directive applies.
The apodosis gives directions which apply to the circumstances delineated.
Several interrelated If-You formulations may be strung together to form an
expanded paragraph unit.[22] The basic nature of this expanded unit, however,
remains essentially the same as the smallest unit, that is, it is a conditional formulation employing the second person address.

The speaker in the Hittite regulations is obviously the king, and those
addressed are the various officials specifically named. A plural address
form is usually employed. It is different with the "Farmer's Almanac." The
farmer speaks to his son (singular) after the manner of the wise counsels.
This raises a question whether the "Farmer's Almanac" belongs with the regulations for officials or with the wise counsels. It is my opinion that it
more nearly fits the category of regulations. In support of this the fol-

lowing may be noted: 1) the wise counsels offer general advice, the almanac offers specific directions; 2) while the almanac may actually derive from an individual farmer giving directions to his son, in its present form it is directed to the farmer in general, not to a specific son, witness the opening lines - "In days of yore a farmer instructed his son (as follows): "; 3) it seems to enjoy official sanction, perhaps that of the king directly. In the Assyrian medical text, it is not clear who the speaker is. The formulations are referred to in the text as "practical prescriptions".

2. Statements of Consequences

Of the If-You formulations in the regulations for officials which are not accompanied by the imperative, all belong to the category of threats and promises.

Threats and Promises. The formulations of this variety resemble to some extent the religious threats and promises in the Old Testament narrative context. They differ in that the religious matters which they treat are of a more specific nature and they are addressed to officials rather than to the people in general. Certain actions are prescribed followed by threats if they are not carried forth. An example is:

> . . . If you do not celebrate them [festivals] with all the
> cattle, sheep, loaves, beer (and) wine set (before the gods),
> and if you, the gods' priests, make a deal with those who
> give all that, you can be sure that the gods will notice what
> is amiss (Temple Officials).[23]

TABLE XXII. THREATS TO OFFICIALS

Ref.		Subject	Num.
Palace Personnel	iii	leather	pl.
Temple Officials	i, 45ff.	festivals	pl.
	i, 50ff.	sacrifices	pl.
	ii, 10ff.	sacrifices	pl.
	iv, 4ff.	young animals	pl.

The purpose of these threats is to coerce compliance with the course of action which is set forth. The protasis envisions a future action of the addressee pertaining to his official duties. The apodosis sets forth the consequences of that action, usually death. As in the case of the other If-You formulations in regulations for officials, the formulations here are not

92

brief and succinct, but are part of lengthier paragraph sized units. Here
also the speaker is the king and those addressed are various officials.

As in the didactic and wisdom literature, so also here the If-You formulations are closely associated with commands and prohibitions. An example
follows:

> Further: You who are leatherworkers of the house of the
> taršipaliyaš, of the house of the appas or the foremen of
> ten among the taršipalaš and you who produce the chariot on
> which the king is to stand, take always oxhides (and) goat-
> skins from the (royal) kitchen! Do not take any other!
>   If you take any other and tell the king about it, it
> is no crime in you. I, the king, will send that abroad or
> give it to my servants.
>   But if you conceal it and it becomes known afterwards,
> they will put you to death together with your wives (and)
> your children (Palace Personnel).[24]

Vassal Treaties

The similarity in form between the ancient Near Eastern vassal treaties,
particularly of the Hittite empire of the late bronze age (1400-1200 B.C.),
and the covenant formulations of the Old Testament is now well known.[25] The
conclusion that the Old Testament covenant formulations are based on the covenant form revealed in the treaties, a form probably in general use in the
second millenium B.C. Near Eastern world, has been widely accepted.[26] More
recently Erhard Gerstenberger has challenged this conclusion, arguing cogently
for a wisdom background for the commandments, tracing their origin to the
words of fathers, tribal heads, wise men, and, secondarily, court officials.[27]

One of the striking features of these treaties is the frequent appearance of If-You formulations. This would seem to offer at least one additional
example of form similarity with the covenant formulations of the Old Testament. If-You formulations occur in at least twelve ancient Near Eastern
treaties.[28]

The speaker and addressee are obviously the two parties to the treaty.
It should be noted that the direct address (grammatical second person) is not
always employed in these ancient treaties. It is not altogether clear what
rationale may have dictated use of the second person in certain treaties and
the third person in others. One possibility is that in cases where the giver

of the treaty had clear superiority over the second party, in this case, the vassal, the second person is employed, whereas in cases in which the parties to the treaty were on more nearly equal footing, the third person was employed. The treaty between Hattusilis and Ramses II,[29] written in third person, would seem to support such a possibility. Only two subdivisions are apparent, directives and threats and promises.

1. Conditional Demands

Directive. Approximately two fifths of the vassal treaty If-You formulations fall into this category. The directive in this context is similar to the directive in Old Testament narrative and to that in regulations for officials in that its word is applied to specific situations. An example of the directive in the vassal treaties is:

> If a fugitive, whether male or female slave, belonging to my country has fled to your land, should you neither seize nor return him but should someone (else) seize him and sur- render him to you, in your prison (you shall put him). When his owner shall come you shall then give him up. Should (šumma) he not be with you, you must provide a man to go in search of him and in whatever city he is abiding he shall arrest him. If he is not abiding (there, he shall say,) "Let the 'town council' name 5 men as his witnesses to (take) the oath of the gods that 'my slave is indeed dwelling among you, then you must inform me.'" (Niqmepa with Ir-im).[30]

TABLE XXIII. VASSAL TREATY DIRECTIVES

Ref.		Subject	Num.
Esarhaddon-Ramataia	ii,136ff	insurrectionists	sg.
Esarhaddon-Baal of Tyre	iii	governor	sg.
Niqmepa-Ir-im	17ff.	right of asylum	sg.
	20ff.	rights of prisoners	sg.
	22-28	fugitive slaves	sg.
	48-52	inter-territorial theft	sg.
	55-60	marauders	sg.
Mursilis II - Niqmepa	10	appearance before the king	sg.
Mursilis II - Duppi-Tessub	10	revolt	sg.
	14	reporting opposition	sg.
	14	executing orders	sg.
	15	accomodating travelers	sg.
	16f.	booty/fugitive	sg.

The protasis sets forth the specific situation to which the directive applies, while the apodosis contains the direction for that situation. Again, as in the regulations for officials, several If-You formulations may be strung together to form a paragraph size unit. Frequently incorporated into this material are threats and promises augmenting the stipulations that have been given.

The subjects treated in the vassal treaty directives pertain largely to inter-territorial matters and cases in which the authority of the great king is threatened. These were matters outside of the direct control of the great king, and for their execution he had to rely upon the loyalty of the vassal. There is some similarity here to the directives of the regulations for officials; for, while they might be under more direct control of the kings, nevertheless, there may have been little evidence had they not performed their duties properly. Therefore, the king had to rely on their good faith, encouraged as it was by his threats and promises.

2. Statements of Consequences

Of the If-You formulations without the imperative, all come under the heading of threats and promises, a category which has already been mentioned in connection with the directive. It is not easy to separate the threats and promises from the directive since the former depends considerably upon the latter for its sense.

Threats and promises. The formulations in this category are similar to the threats and promises in Old Testament narrative context and in the regulations for officials in that the intent is to warn of the consequences of certain future courses of action through promises which would reward the desired action. An example of the threats and promises in the vassal treaties is:

> If anyone should press you hard, Duppi-Tessub, or (if) anyone should revolt against you, (if) you then write to the king of the Hatti land, and the king of the Hatti land dispatches foot soldiers and charioteers to your aid - if you treat them in an unfair manner , you act in disregard of the gods of the oath (Mursilis with Duppi-Tessub).[31]

TABLE XXIV. VASSAL TREATY THREATS AND PROMISES

Ref.		Subject	Num.
Esarhaddon-Ramataia	vi, 414	royal documents	sg.
	vii,513	transgression of treaty	sg.
Ashurnirari V-Mati'ilu	iii	asylum to enemy	sg.
Bar-ga'ayah-Mati'el	I	fulfillment of treaty	sg.

(Table XXIV. cont.)

	I	military aid	sg.
	I	fulfillment of treaty	sg.
	I	provisions	sg.
	IIB	obedience, loyalty	sg.
	III	fulfillment of treaty	sg.
	III	refugees	sg.
	III	fulfillment of treaty	sg.
	III	fulfillment of treaty	sg.
	III	good will	sg.
	III	treason	sg.
Huqqanas		evil actions	sg.
Mursilis II-Manapa-Dattas	4-5	fulfillment of treaty	sg.
Muwatallis-Alaksandus	13	rebellion	sg.
Mursilis II-Niqmepa	20	military aid	sg.
Tudhaliyas IV-Ulmi-Teshub		fulfillment of treaty	sg.
Mursilis II-Duppi-Teshub	9	military aid	sg.
	10	military aid	sg.
	11	treatment of Hittite soldiers	sg.
	13	deportees	sg.
	14	executing orders	sg.
	15	accomodating travelers	sg.
	16	booty	sg.
Suppiluliumas-Mattiwaza		fulfillment of treaty	sg.
		fulfillment of treaty	sg.

The protasis sets forth a future situation pertaining to the addressee's action in carrying forth the treaty obligations. In most instances a specific case is described, as in the example given above. There are, however, a few instances in which a general condition of transgressing the treaty is set forth as in the following example:

> If you, Mattiwaza, the prince, and (you) the sons of the Hurri country do not fulfill the words of this treaty, may the gods, the lords of the oath, blot you out, (you) Mattiwaza and (you) the Hurri men together with your country, your wives and all that you have (Suppiluliumas with Mattiwaza).[32]

In the apodosis there is a variety of rather vague threats and promises, mostly threats. While the phraseology varies, in nearly all instances the wrath of the gods of the treaty is threatened against the addressee if he fails to live up to his obligations. This is true also in those cases in which betrayal of the oath is mentioned, since breach of the oath was understood to bring about the wrath of the gods. In only three instances is reference made to the wrath of the king and two of these are promises of peace rather than threats.

Again it should be noted that If-You formulations in the vassal treaties are closely associated with You-Shall forms, as in the following example:

> Or if the king of the Hatti land is getting the better
> of a country and puts them to flight, and they come to
> your country, if then you desire to take anything from
> them, ask the king of the Hatti land for it! You shall
> not take it on your own! If you lay hand on it by yourself
> or conceal it, (you act in disregard of the oath) (Mursilis
> with Duppi-Tessub).[33]

Summary

In the comparative Near Eastern materials no new groupings of If-You formulations appear. Nearly all of them fall into three categories already recognized in the Old Testament material, directive, counsel, and threats and promises.

In the didactic and wisdom literature the largest number of formulations are directives. The remainder, with but minor exceptions, come under the heading of counsel. Noteworthy for their virtual absence in the didactic and wisdom literature are the threats and promises which are prevalent in regulations for officials and in vassal treaties. It is of the nature of wisdom to warn of consequences, as in the counsel, but not to threaten (or promise). The persuasion of the wise makes its appeal to reason rather than to emotion. Furthermore, compliance with the counsel gained reward for the addressee, whereas in other cases the gain goes to the speaker.

The regulations for officials comprise a category which comes close to being law. Again, two groupings stand out, the directive, which is the largest, and the threats and promises. There is a small group of threats and promises which seem closely associated with the directives, giving support to them. It will be noted that there are no threats and promises in the military regulations. There is no need for this kind of persuasion in cases where the immediate threat of the king's wrath is present. Threats and promises are usually employed in areas where enforcement of a regulation or command is difficult if not impossible.

In the vassal treaties the same two groupings are encountered; however, the threats and promises outnumber the directives. The reason for this probably has to do with a greater need for persuasion in the case of the vassal treaties. In the latter there is a greater distance between the speaker and the addressee, whereas in the regulations for officials the threat of the king's presence may have moderated the need for additional persuasion. Here again the close association between directive and threats and promises should be noted.

The If-You formulations in the comparative Near Eastern material are words of sages and of kings, mostly of the latter. They are words closely associated with commands and prohibitions in You-Shall style, augmenting them and giving them additional persuasive support. At times it does not appear as though they could be separated from the commands and prohibitions they accompany.

The address may be to one or to many, but in either case there is no confusion about the meaning of the number. In most cases the singular address is employed, and it is clear that a singular meaning is intended. When the sage speaks to his pupil, he speaks to an individual. When a king speaks to his vassal, he likewise speaks to an individual. Whenever a plural address is employed, it is clear that a group is being addressed. This is particularly evident in regulations for officials.

V. THE ORIGIN OF LEGAL
IF-YOU FORMULATIONS

How old are the If-You formulations in Israel? When were they introduced into law? What is the extent of the period of their usage? Did they
undergo any changes during this period? Some help in answering these questions is gained from the comparative material.

A. Relations Between Major Categories

Of the five categories previously analyzed, only the directives, the
counsels, and the threats and promises are repeated frequently enough in the
Near Eastern material to serve as a basis of inquiry into the problem of the
inclusion of If-You formulations in law. Of these, the directive recurs with
the greatest frequency. As an If-You form it is rare in the prophetic material. In its most primitive occurrence in narrative contexts it is applied to
a variety of specific, unrepeatable situations.

The directive in Old Testament wisdom material is similar to that found
in the wise counsels of the ancient Near East. Only the singular address is
employed. In both contexts the directive constitutes the largest number of
the If-You formulations, and in both contexts they deal with situations of a
repeatable character. The situations envisioned are mostly relational matters, and indications are given for the proper mode of social behavior. They
share a similar character with most other wisdom sayings in that they are the
precipitate of a long period of development. The movement from specific situations in narrative contexts to general situations in wisdom contexts reveals
a degree of development which is doubtless attributable to a process of reflection. Reflection is required in extending what began as a specific direction for a particular circumstance to a broader context or class of events.

The appearance of the directive in regulations for officials, closely
associated with formulations in You-Shall style, reveals a more specialized
use of the form. The subjects treated are more specific in character than
those in wisdom; however, they, too, refer to classes of repeatable events

and actions. These formulations provide the closest link between the primitive directive and those If-You formulations in law which employ the imperative. They are closer to the juridical formulations than to any other group.
The juridical formulations like the instructions to officials are addressed
to a special group of people concerning specific matters of special interest
to them. While there are few juridical instructions in If-You style in the
Near Eastern material, several texts do indicate that judicial officials
(including military officials) were usually instructed in second-person style.[1]

The humanitarian, ceremonial, and holy-war If-You formulations have a
similarity in form with the directive to officials; however, they differ from
the latter in that their address is more general. Specific groups of people
are not singled out. It is true, second-person ceremonial regulations in Near
Eastern material are addressed to specific functionaries.[2] Certain of the Old
Testament ceremonial formulations are similarly addressed to special groups,[3]
but the majority in their present form are addressed generally to Israel.

The vassal treaties represent another specialized usage of the directive.
They too denote specific areas of concern and are intended to apply to all
future situations of the kind specified. Here too the king is the speaker,
but one individual is addressed.

Of the three categories, directives, counsels, and threats and promises,
the counsels occur with least frequency. They appear in Old Testament narratives and in Israelite and other wisdom contexts. In a narrative context the
counsel is a word of advice concerning a particular, non-repetitive situation.
The tone is persuasive, appealing to the reasonableness of the observation
given. In wisdom contexts the counsel shifts focus to general, repetitive
situations. Here too the tone is one of persuasion, appealing to the reasonableness of the observations of the wise, and for this reason it seems an
especially appropriate vehicle for wise instruction. This kind of counsel is
clearly in evidence in I Kings 12:6f. in which it is said that Rehoboam took
counsel with Solomon's elders. The elders are represented as having given
advice to Rehoboam in the If-You instructional style: "If thou wilt be a
servant to this people today and serve them, and answer them and speak good

words to them, then they will be thy servants for ever." It appears then that the If-You counsel is a special form adopted and developed by the wise in putting forth their advice and counsel. It does not occur in Israelite law.

The third category of If-You formulations which are found with some regularity are the threats and promises. This group is absent in Old Testament and Near Eastern wisdom contexts. The reason for this absence in wisdom has already been noted, namely that the persuasion of the wise tended more toward reason than toward the emotional appeal of the threats and promises. In their most primitive form the threats and promises concern non-religious matters between individuals, and they appear in Old Testament narrative contexts. As previously noted, their purpose is to warn of the consequences of certain future actions or to exert pressure on future actions through promises which would reward the desired action, thus attempting to influence the behavior of the addressee. Religious threats and promises likewise are found in narrative contexts. They represent a specialized use of the threats and promises, persuading and encouraging loyalty to Yahweh and observance of his commandments. In this respect they seem quite close to the threats and promises in the legal portions of the Old Testament. They differ in that the threats and promises in Old Testament law are addressed to Israel in general whereas the religious threats and promises in narratives are addressed either to Israel in general or to specific individuals such as Solomon or Jeroboam. When Israel is addressed the plural is always employed. As previously noted, many of the religious threats and promises in narratives have been attributed to the Deuteronomist.

Threats and promises are also found in prophetic material. It is not clear that they are indigenous prophetic forms, however, since it has been shown that they belong to expansions of prophetic oracles. They are particularly evident in the Book of Jeremiah, and there they are usually cast in plural address form. The deuteronomistic influence in the Book of Jeremiah has been remarked before.[4] For this reason and because the plural address is employed in other deuteronomistic contexts, it seems reasonable to attribute these sections in Jeremiah to a deuteronomistic editorial process.

In the regulations for officials threats and promises are interspersed with directives, giving support to the latter. Divine sanction is introduced in at least one instance.[5] In the vassal treaties the threats and promises typically invoke divine sanction. This is threatened on the basis that if the stipulations of the treaty are broken one acts in disregard of the gods of the oath. The use of threats and promises in Israelite law follows a similar pattern. They are interspersed among the laws, among If-You and You-Shall styled laws particularly, giving them extra force.

B. The Background of Legal
If-You Formulations

The recognition that there are several If-You forms, some of which have very specialized functions, complicates the question of the appearance of If-You formulations in Israelite law. The survey of the Old Testament narratives has shown the If-You formulations to be fundamental, natural speech patterns. Certainly, the narrative contexts furnish the broadest linguistic spectrum and the most diffuse sample for investigation. It supplies the most primitive examples of If-You formulations in terms of linguistic phenomena. That all five of the categories appear in narratives is probably due to the primary nature of the language in that context. But at what point can it be said that the If-You formulation has moved beyond the stage of primitive speech and become more specialized forms (Gattungen)? Among the forms employed in ancient Israel to give expression to laws and regulations for the community, the If-You formulations recur in all the major legal sections of the Pentateuch and are particularly numerous in Deuteronomy. This fact alone clearly indicates that such formulations had been in use over a long period of time. The fact that they were not regularly employed in any of the extant ancient Near Eastern codes of law suggests that they have been borrowed from an area of life other than that of law codes. The other possible conclusion, that they are indigenous legal forms, appears unwarranted.

The fact has already been established that in the narratives the If-You formulations are usually the words of authorities. In the didactic and wisdom literature, in regulations for officials, in the vassal treaties, and in Deuteronomy a close relationship between If-You styled demands and You-Shall styled demands (the commands and prohibitions) has been observed. If the protasis of the If-You styled directive is removed, the apodosis stands alone quite clearly as a command or prohibition. If, for example, the protasis in II Kings 9:15 is removed, the following remains: "Let no one slip out of the city to go and tell the news in Jezreel." Clearly, the apodosis conveys the most essential information. Specific conditions may be proposed for the application of a command to a particular circumstance or for the limiting of it to a particular class of events. Modification of this kind reflects a process or rationalization. While the direct quality of the command itself is unaltered, there does seem to be some change in tone, a change which possibly is purely subjective, a result of the listener's mental association of the If-You style particularly with the If-You counsel. In the latter there is a marked persuasive tone.

Gerstenberger has cogently argued that the You-Shall styled demands (the commands and prohibitions) originate in a family ethos. While there are no If-You directives in their present form which reveal an altogether clear relation to a family ethos, nevertheless, it is reasonable to assume such a point of origin. The clear association of the directives with You-Shall commands and prohibitions already suggests that possibility, granted, of course, the accuracy of Gerstenberger's argument. The latter's position is strengthened by the many admonitions in the Old Testament wisdom material which indicate that parents had primary responsibility for the education of the young. The word tôrāh is frequently employed to designate this educational function. An example of this usage is in Prov. 1:8 -

> Hear, my son, the instruction (musār) of thy father,
> and do not reject thy mother's torah.

Here tôrāh is paralled by musār and apparently has the meaning of 'instruction' in a broad sense. In Prov. 3:1 tôrāh is paralled by miswotai:

> My son, do not forget my tôrāh, and let thy heart
> keep my commandments (miswotai).

The same phenomenon is apparent in Prov. 6:20 -

> My son, keep the commandments (miswat) of thy father,

> and do not forsake thy mother's tôrāh.

Other similar passages could be cited.[6] In Prov. 28:7, one who observes his
father's tôrāh is contrasted to the companion of gluttonous men. Thus, it
seems clear enough that within the family there took place an instructional
process designated tôrāh which was closely associated with commands and prohibitions. It seems reasonable that instructions in If-You style were part of
this process. Some support for such a contention comes from the Egyptian
didactic texts, which contain a large number of If-You formulations, and from
the Words of Ahiqar. While these didactic texts are rather formalized literary endeavors, nevertheless, they are cast in the form of instructions of
parents to children. They possibly reflect the instructional patterns of a
more primitive family ethos. A similar phenomenon can be observed in the
Book of Proverbs, which is at least in part cast in the form of instructions
of parents to children. Of particular note is the frequent use of the address,
"my son", which introduces many of the instructions and which is also used to
introduce If-You styled demands.

From this base in domestic paideia, If-You formulations were taken up by
special functionaries. Among the wise it was particularly favored. Its use
in wisdom literature can be observed over a long period of time, from the
fifth Egyptian dynasty (ca. 2450 B.C.)[7] through the period of the late Israelite monarchy.[8] The directive was most commonly employed in the wisdom
writings, but the counsel was given special attention by the wise and became
their special way of instruction through statement of consequences.

There are indications that If-You formulations were taken up also by
priests. Here they were employed in the imparting of ceremonial instructions,
perhaps to the laity, perhaps to cultic officials. The prophets also employed If-You formulations to a limited extent as exhortations and warnings.

Royal speech reveals extensive usage of If-You formulations. The If-
You formulations, particularly the directive accompanied by threats and
promises, was employed as an appropriate tool in setting forth instructions
for numerous officials. The authority of the king is reflected in the use of
the second-person style. While the instructions to officials predate the Old
Testament material, it is nevertheless only a short step from the instruc-

tions to the If-You formulations in Old Testament law, particularly the juridical formulations which display the closest similarity. Like the Near
Eastern instructions to officials, they too were addressed to a particular
group of officials and set forth specific instructions concerning their functions. The instructions to judicial officials in the Near Eastern material
carry the authority of the ruler; indeed, they are represented as royal speech.
Is there any reason to suspect that similar instructions to judicial officials
in Israelite law do not carry such state authority? Certainly, from a practical standpoint such authority was necessary to the effective maintenance of
a judicial system such as that envisioned in Deuteronomy. Furthermore, the fact
that the form of the juridical If-You formulations is unique suggests that they
have been transmitted with virtually little change from their original state.

It would doubtless be inaccurate to say that all If-You formulations in
Old Testament legal material are the result of one cause. If-You formulations
are used in Old Testament law over a long period of time. They are found
already in the Book of the Covenant and in all subsequent legal strata. Deuteronomy, however, shows a great preference for the If-You style. To what or
to whom may we attribute this preference?

Several questions have been applied to the Book of Deuteronomy in order
to solve the problem of its history and the identity of the circles responsible for its creation. Three of these questions stand out: 1) the question
of historical allusions in the book 2) the question of style, and 3) the
question of point of view reflected in its composition as a whole, and in its
parts. The If-You formulations have little to offer in the area of historical
relationships, with the exception that they are employed in laws pertaining
to centralization. Of greater importance is the fact that they are integral
to the style of Deuteronomy and are also prominent in those areas of interest
expressed in the book which give it its special character.

One widely held theory has been that the parenetic style of Deuteronomy
derives from an actual oral promulgation.[9] O. Bächli has argued that the
homiletic style of Deuteronomy derives from the royal preaching of the law.[10]
He points to the law of the king in Deut. 17:14-20 in support of his position.
The king appears to have been charged with the responsibility of reading and

interpreting the law in public. He points to the activities of Joshua, Samuel, and Solomon in this regard as evidence that this law had actual basis in fact. It appears, however, that the deuteronomic material reveals much more a conscious literary effort. Moshe Weinfeld has recently shown how the orations in deuteronomic literature can be explained as programmatic speeches produced by court scribes at their writing tables.[11] One additional stylistic criterion is the mixture of If-You forms in Deuteronomy, specifically the mixture of directives with threats and promises. While Deuteronomy shares this characteristic with other legal sections, it is particularly prominent in Deuteronomy. The same phenomenon has been observed as a stylistic peculiarity in the regulations for officials and in the vassal treaties, both of which are products of royal courts.

The evidence from the comparative material points away from any typically cultic setting for most If-You styled formulations unless the royal court be considered a cultic entity. There are some ceremonial formulations, obviously priestly in origin, but these are fairly isolated and are also quite different from those found in Deuteronomy. Most of the If-You styled formulations in comparative material are found in texts emanating from royal courts or in wisdom texts, many of which are also related to royal courts, though perhaps indirectly. Recently E. W. Nicholson has argued that the parenetic style of Deuteronomy points for its origin to a cultic setting, and is specifically to be assigned to prophetic circles originating in the north.[12] The relative infrequency of If-You formulations in prophetic speech has already been noted. While this fact is scarcely sufficient to negate Nicholson's thesis, it does in some measure stand over against it.

When the question of point of view is posed, additional support is given to the possibility of a royal court background for the If-You formulations in Deuteronomy. Attention has been drawn to the fact that If-You formulations permeate the interests which give Deuteronomy its own peculiar character and that to remove these formulations would radically alter the book. The question then posed is whether these interests are such that they would fit a ruling class ethos. The centralization program is clearly in the interests of the monarchy. It offered greater control of cultic activities and a platform from which to put forward desired reforms. It is difficult to see that it would have served priestly interests outside of Jerusalem.

Another major element in Deuteronomy is the humanitarian concern. Humanitarian morality is not confined to the Old Testament. On the contrary, it is found frequently in the literature of the Ancient Near East, particularly in the didactic literature. Of this literature, perhaps no other example is so richly endowed with humanitarian morality as the "Instruction of Amen-em-ope". The comparison of the "Instruction of Amen-em-ope" with Prov. 22:17-24 has been well known since first treated by Erman in 1924. The following example reveals this humanitarian moral tendency:

> Chapter 20
>
>> Do not confuse a man in the law court,
>> Nor divert the righteous man.
>> Give not thy attention (only) to him
>>   clothed in white,
>> Nor give consideration to him that is
>>   unkempt.
>> Do not accept the bribe of a powerful man,
>> Nor oppress for him the disabled.
>> As for justice, the great reward of god,
>> He gives it to whom he will . . . (ANET, p. 424).

The decidedly humanitarian tone of the Egyptian instructional literature is quite apparent. Moreover, this humanitarian morality is admonished along religious lines with frequent reference to divinity. Had the instructions been written in the form of law codes, they would for the most part have appeared as commands and prohibitions. In so far as the translation reflects the original form, the majority of the instructions have a preceptive tone; for example: "Injure not a man . . ." (Ch. 13). In two instances the If-You formulation occurs, this in Chapter 13 line 7 and Chapter 28 line 1.[13]

The great body of that literature which was discovered on the site of ancient Ugarit takes the form of epic poetry. Within this material there are allusions to the existence of a humanitarian moral outlook. In that portion of the Keret story wherein Keret covets the throne for himself there is the following:

>> Keret returns to his former estate;
> He sits upon the throne of kingship;
>> Upon the dais, the seat of authority.
> Now, Yassib sits in the palace,
>> And his inward parts do instruct him:

> "Go unto thy father, Yassib;
> Go unto thy fa (ther) and speak,
> Repeat unto Ke (ret the Noble):
> 'List and incline (thine ear).
> (one couplet unintelligible)
> Thou hast let thy hand fall into mischief.
> Thou judgest not the cause of the widow,
> Nor adjudicat'st the case of the wretched.
> . . . .
> Descend from the kingship - I'll reign;
> From thine authority - I'll sit enthroned.'"
> . . . .
> Driv'st not out them that prey on the poor;
> Feed'st not the fatherless before thee,
> The widow behind thy back.[14]

Here again is the humanitarian moral motif concerning the oppressed classes.
It was the king's duty to protect the less fortunate in the land. Yassib's
argument is that his father is not acting the part of king in this respect.
The "Legend of Aqhat" repeats this same theme in its relation to the king.[15]

A number of inscriptions lend credence to the argument that the royal
office entailed certain humanitarian responsibilities. Inscriptions are generally of two types, they either extol the great conquests of the king and his
mighty valor or they claim his wise and humane rule.[16]

The following conclusions with regard to the humanitarian morality of
the ancient Near East stand out: 1) It is widespread, found in many different
spheres; 2) It is regarded as a virtue of a great king; 3) It is frequently
admonished along religious lines, the king usually being regarded as the rep-
resentative of the god on earth;[17] 4) It is frequently accompanied by motive
clauses; and 5) The tendency is more toward persuasion than toward coercion.
Furthermore, this humanitarian morality, as it has been transmitted, is essentially a development of a settled society. In a nomadic clan society there is
a strong obligation to protect weak and oppressed members.[18] The widow, the
orphan, the poor are cared for within the clan. It is only with the break-
down of clan society that there develops a need for special attention to these
matters. In addition, the frequent mention of landmarks and property in general, and the mention of justice in the gate points to a settled, agricultural
society. It appears then that the present formulation of this humanitarian
morality is not a product of Israel's wilderness period.

The ideology of Holy War is another concern which has made a deep impress on the deuteronomic legislation. Von Rad first drew attention to this feature of the Book of Deuteronomy, pointing to the number of laws on war in the book and to the war ideology permeating several of the speeches.[19] He held that whoever composed the book apparently stood within the cultic and sacral traditions of the old Yahwistic amphictyony. According to von Rad, country Levites were responsible for the composition of the book, but, as already observed in the previous analysis, in Deuteronomy the holy-war traditions have undergone a marked desacralization and reflect the humanitarian ideal which motivates much of the other legislation.

To whom may Deuteronomy's politico-military nature be attributed? Surely the monarchy was concerned with Israel's secure place among the nations. This, it may be recalled, was the motivating factor in the creation of the monarchy in Israel, for Saul was first anointed as a nāgîd, a military leader.[20] There seems no reason to doubt that the old traditions were as accessable to the central government as they would have been to any other sector of Israelite society. In particular, the deferment regulations seem to be closely connected with the monarchy.

Two objections have been lodged against the monarchy as the party standing behind the refurbishing of these old traditions in Deuteronomy: 1) That none of the war laws give the king the authoritative role in the conduct of war which in fact was his, and 2) that the law of the king in Deut. 17:14-20 is not favorable toward the monarchy. It may not, however, have been necessary to state the obvious concerning the king's function in war. In addition, it is not necessarily true that the law of the king should be taken negatively, particularly in light of the generally positive attitude toward kingship expressed in the Deuteronomic literature.[21] Syria-Palestine was a rain culture. Prosperity did not depend upon a highly centralized, autocratic monarchy. In Syria-Palestine it is clear that the kings had more the character of local chieftains whose authority was circumscribed by a state council whose members were recruited from the ranks of the rich agricultural and commercial families.[22] A similar body existed in Israel, and they are usually identified as elders. In the period before the monarchy local government was concentrated in the hands of the elders. They chose and anointed the first kings[23] and even after the appearance of the monarchy they retained a certain amount of local governmental authority.[24] They were called together in times of crisis by the king as representatives of their local communities. In I Kings 12:6f. Rehoboam takes counsel with the elders who had stood before Solomon as part of the ruling establishment. It appears, therefore, that power was shared with a kind of state council, and it was probably this group which effectively limited the power of the king.

The juridical concerns set forth in If-You style have already been revealed as concerns of the ruling class. They are similar to the regulations for officials in that they are addressed to a specific group of officials. The authority implied in the juridical formulations strongly suggests state involvement. Even when specifically religious concerns are treated, they are not devoid of state interest. The subjects treated, false worship, idolatry, were important to the maintenance of the community and for this reason became state concerns. One problem in particular which remains unresolved is that of the special position accorded the Levites in Deuteronomy, e.g., their inclusion in the class of personae miserabiles, their position as judicial officials, and their access to the central shrine.

Summary

The If-You styled directives in Old Testament law are clearly related to the commands and prohibitions. They are a development from the latter under the aegis of a process of reflection and rationalization, modifying them for specific cases. We have assumed because of this relationship to the commands and prohibitions that they originate in the same ethos, namely the family ethos suggested by Gerstenberger. The form is then taken up by special functionaries including the wise, priests, prophets, kings and elders. It was a style particularly favored by the wise as a vehicle for their instructions. This ancient instructional tradition finally came into focus in the royal courts where it was employed in the instruction of officials and in the broader context of law.

Stylistic and ideological considerations pertaining to the If-You formulations in Deuteronomy strongly suggest a royal court <u>milieu</u>. Beyond this a more specific designation of the circles behind the composition of Deuteronomy cannot be obtained on the basis of an analysis of the If-You formulations alone.

CONCLUSION

As described in the introduction, the task of this investigation was to analyze the conditional formulations in Israelite law which employ a second-person address, the If-You formulations. Briefly, the problem may be restated: first, do these formulations form a) a separate recognizable category of law, b) a conflation of other types, c) subdivisions of other types, or d) a combination of these possibilities? Second, do they serve some particular function in Israelite law? Previous treatments have proceeded on a fairly narrow basis with little or no attention to comparative material. There has been a tendency to regard the If-You formulations as a late conflation of the ordinary casuistic "If" form and the "You-Shall" form.

The investigation of the If-You formulations has revealed that such formulations in Israelite law are not a late mixture of types, but an old form which had been in use over a long period of time, appearing in all the major legal corpora of the Old Testament. Even in the juridical formulations which seem to have some affinity with the ordinary casuistic "If" forms, the form is a result of the situation out of which they come, not the result of a literary mixture. Secondly, the investigation has shown that the If-You formulations in law are closely related to the commands and prohibitions in "You-Shall" style and are a development from the latter under the aegis of a process of reflection and rationalization.

The investigation of the conditional sentences employing second person address also has revealed not one literary type, but several. The basic categories established are five in number. These have been grouped further on the basis of the presence of the imperative:

Conditional Demands (with imperative)
    1. Request
    2. Directives

Statements of Consequences (without imperative)
    3. Agreements
    4. Threats and Promises
    5. Counsels

113

Three of these categories can be traced from their setting in primitive speech
to specialized usages. Directives are prominent in wisdom and in legal context. Counsels are a particular device of the wise, who employed this form
in their instruction and advice. Threats and promises are employed in instructions to officials, in vassal treaties, and finally in Israelite law; in all
these contexts this category functions as a support to directives and demands
in other styles.

In legal contexts, If-You formulations function in certain specific
areas. They are employed in laws dealing with <u>ceremonial</u> matters, reflecting
priestly instructions to worshipers. They are employed in <u>holy-war</u> laws,
found exclusively in Deuteronomy. They are particularly prominent in <u>humani-</u>
<u>tarian</u> legislation, an area in which persuasion is important for the effec-
tiveness of the law. The choice of the If-You style in promulgating humanitarian laws is not at all coincidental. There existed an age-old tradition of
instruction in Israel as well as in the other lands of the ancient Near East.
The If-You style had served as a vehicle of persuasion since early times. It
was a form particularly accepted in court circles for edification and teaching.
If-You formulations are employed in the promulgation of <u>juridical</u> laws and in
this area they constitute a special category. While they exhibit some similarities to other legal types, their form emerges from the fact that they are
addressed to judicial officials. In this regard they resemble instructions
to officials in ancient Near Eastern texts. They represent a stage in the
development of law in which the state is assuming responsibility for certain
criminal matters which had previously been handled otherwise. In particular,
they are utilized in the regulation of the juridical process itself. As
threats and promises, If-You formulations function as <u>parenetic</u> additions to
law, but are structurally different from laws as such.

One striking feature of the If-You formulations in law is the frequency
of their appearance in Deuteronomy. The If-You styled portions could be removed from Deuteronomy only by doing great harm to the essential nature of
the book. The If-You formulations are so much a part of the Deuteronomic
style that one cannot disregard them when approaching the question of the

origin of Deuteronomy. In this study no attempt has been made to cover the many questions concerning the provenance of Deuteronomy. In particular, attention has been drawn to the Near Eastern didactic and wisdom literature, instructions to officials, and vassal treaties, which indicate a royal court background for If-You formulations. Further, it has been shown that one stylistic peculiarity of Deuteronomy is the mixture of If-You directives with If-You threats and promises. The same phenomenon has been observed in the instructions to officials and in the vassal treaties, both of which emanate from royal courts. Also it has been suggested that the particular subjects which are treated in If-You style, i.e. humanitarian concerns, centralization, holy war, and juridical matters, can be seen as interests of the ruling class.

Recently, considerable evidence has been brought forth which indicates that wisdom and law have closely related backgrounds. The phenomenon of the If-You formulations furnishes additional evidence in support of an at least partial connection between law and wisdom.

A SELECTED BIBLIOGRAPHY

Alp, Sedat, "Military Instructions of the Hittite King Tuthaliya IV."
Belleten, XI (1947), 383-414.

Alt, Albrecht, Kleine Schriften zur Geschichte des Volkes Israels. vol. I,
München (C. H. Beck'sche), 1953.

Bächli, O., Israel und die Volker: eine Studie zum Deuteronomium. Zürich,
1962.

Begrich, J., "Die Priesterliche Tora." Werden und Wesen des A. T., ed. J.
Hempel. Berlin (Töpelmann), 1936.

Bentzen, Aage, Introduction to the Old Testament. 2 vols., Copenhagen (G. E.
C. Gad), 1961.

Boecker, Hans Jochen, Redeformen des Rechtsleben im Alten Testament.
Neukirchen (Neukirchener Verlag), 1964.

Buis, Pierre, et Jacques Leclercq, Le Deutéronome. Paris (Librairie LeCoffre),
1963.

Cazelles, Henri, Etudes sur le Code de L'Alliance. Paris (Letouzey et Ané),
1946.

_____, "Passages in the Singular Within Discourse in the Plural of
Dt. 1-4." CBQ, XXIX (1967), 207-219.

Cornhill, C. H., Introduction to the Canonical Books of the Old Testament,
trans. G. H. Box. London, 1907.

Crenshaw, J. L., "Method in Determining Wisdom Influence upon 'Historical'
Literature." JBL, LXXXVIII (1969), 129-142.

Daube, David, Studies in Biblical Law. Cambridge (Cambridge University Press),
1947.

Davies, Norman de Garis, ed., "The Installation of the Vizier." The Tomb of
Rekh-mi-re at Thebes. vol. I, New York, 1948.

Driver, S. R., A Critical and Exegetical Commentary on Deuteronomy, The
International Critical Commentary. New York (Scribners), 1895.

Eissfeldt, Otto, The Old Testament: An Introduction. New York (Harper and
Row), 1965.

Elliger, Karl, Leviticus, Handbuch zum Alten Testament. vol. 4, Tübingen
(J. C. B. Mohr), 1966.

Fensham, F. Charles, "Widow, Orphan and the Poor in Ancient Near Eastern Legal
and Wisdom Literature." JNES, XXI (1962), 129-137.

Feucht, Christian, Untersuchungen zum Heiligkeitsgesetz. Berlin (Evangelische
Verlagsanstalt), 1964.

Fohrer, George, "Das sogenannte apodiktisch formulierte Recht und der Dekalog."
Kerygma und Dogma, II (1965).

Gardiner, Alan, Egyptian Grammar. 3rd. ed. Oxford (Oxford University Press), 1964.

Gemser, B., "The Importance of the Motive Clause in Old Testament Law." Supplements to Vetus Testamentum, vol. I, Copenhagen, 1953, 50-66.

_____, "The Instructions of 'Onchsheshonqy and Biblical Wisdom Literature." Supplements to Vetus Testamentum, vol. VIII, Leiden, 1960, 102-128.

Gese, Hartmut, "Beobachtungen zum Stil alttestamentlicher Rechtssätze." Theologische Literaturzeitung, LXXXIV (1960), cols. 147-150.

Gerstenberger, Erhard, "Covenant and Commandment." JBL, LXXXIV (1965), 38-51.

_____, Wesen und Herkunft des apodiktischen Rechts. Neukirchen (Neukirchener Verlag), 1965.

Gesenius, Kautzsch, Cowley, Hebrew Grammar. Oxford (Clarendon Press), 1910.

Gevirtz, Stanley, "West-Semetic Curses and the Problem of the Origins of Hebrew Law." VT, II (1961), 137-158.

Glanville, S. R. K., Catalogue of Demotic Papyri in the British Museum, vol. II, The Instruction of 'Onchsheshonqy, Part I, London (Trustees of the British Museum), 1955.

Goetze, A., The Laws of Eshnunna, Annual of the American Schools of Oriental Research. XXXI, New Haven, 1956.

Grapow, Herman, Untersuchungen über die Altagyptischen Medizinischen Papyri. Leipzig (J. C. Hinrichs's Che Buchhandlung), 1935.

Gray, G. B., Sacrifice in the Old Testament. Oxford (Clarendon), 1925.

Hammershaimb, E., "On the Ethics of the Old Testament Prophets." Supplements to Vetus Testamentum. vol. VII, Leiden (E. J. Brill), 1960.

Hempel, Johannes, Die Schichten des Deuteronomiums. Leipzig (R. Voigtländer), 1914.

Horst, S. R., Das Privilegrecht Jahwes. Göttingen, 1930.

Jepsen, Alfred, Untersuchungen zum Bundesbuch. Stuttgart (W. Kohlhammer), 1927.

Jirku, Anton, Das weltliche Recht im Alten Testament: Stilgeschichtliche und recht vergleichends Studien zu den juristischen Gestzen des Pentateuchs. Gutersloth, 1927.

Kayatz, Christa, Studien zu Proverbien 1-9. Neukirchen (Neukirchener Verlag), 1966.

Kilian, Rudolf, Literarkritische und Formgeschichtliche Untersuchung des Heiligkeitsgesetzes. Bonn (Peter Hanstein Verlag), 1963.

_____, "Apodiktisches und kasuistiches Recht im Licht agyptischer Analogien." Biblische Zeitschrift. VII (1963), 185-202.

Koch, Klaus, Die Priesterschrift von Exodus 25 bis Leviticus 16. Göttingen (Vandenhoeck and Ruprecht), 1959.

Kornfeld, Walter, _Studien zum Heiligkeitsgesetz_. Wien (Herder), 1952.

Kramer, S. N., _The Sumerians: Their History, Culture, and Character_. Chicago (Chicago University Press), 1963.

Krause, Hans-Helmut, _Das Deuteronomium im der wissenschaftlichen Bearbeitung des 19. und 20. Jahrhunderts nebst 2 Anhangen der Bericht 2 Kg. 22/23 und die Stilgattung in den Gesetzen des Dtn_. Breslau, 1931.

Liebesny, Herbert, "The Administration of Justice in Nuzi." _JAOS_. LXIII (1943).

McCarthy, D. J., _Treaty and Covenant, Analecta Biblica_. Rome (Pontifical Biblical Institute), 1963.

MacKenzie. R. A. F., _Two Forms of Israelite Law_. Toronto (Pontifical Biblical Institute), 1961.

_____, "The Forms of Israelite Law: A Comparative Study of Some Word Patterns in the Pentateuch." unpub. diss., Rome, 1949.

Manley, G. T., _The Book of the Law_. Grand Rapids (Eerdmanns), 1957.

Mendenhall, G. E., _Law and Covenant in Israel and in the Ancient Near East_. Pittsburgh (The Biblical Colloquium), 1955.

_____, "Covenant." _IDB_. vol. I, 714-723.

Mowinckel, Sigmumd, _Le Decalogue_. Paris, 1927.

_____, "Zur Geschichte des Dekalogs." _ZAW_. LV (1937), 218-234.

Morgenstern, Julian, "The Book of the Covenant." _Hebrew Union College Annual_, V (1928), 1-151, VII (1930), 19-258, VIII-IX (1931-32), 1-150.

Naveh, J., "A Hebrew Letter from the Seventh Century B.C." _IEJ_, X (1960), 129-139.

Neufeld, E., _The Hittite Laws_. London (Luzac), 1951.

Nicholson, E. W., _Deuteronomy and Tradition_. Philadelphia (Fortress), 1967.

Nielsen, Eduard, _The Ten Commandments in New Perspective_. _SBT_. 2nd series, Naperville (Alec R. Allenson), 1968.

Noth, Martin, _Exodus: A Commentary_. Philadelphia (Westminster), 1962.

_____, _Leviticus: A Commentary_. Philadelphia (Westminster), 1965.

_____, "The Laws in the Pentateuch." _The Laws in the Pentateuch and Other Essays_. London (Oliver and Boyd) 1966.

Östborn, Gunnar, _Tora in the Old Testament: A Semantic Study_. Lund (Håkan Ohlssons Boktryckeri), 1945.

Pfeiffer, R. H., _Introduction to the Old Testament_. New York (Harper and Son), 1941.

Ploeg, J. van der, "Studies in Hebrew Law III." _CBQ_, XIII (1951), 28-43.

Ploger, Joseph G., _Literarkritische, formgeschichtiche und strilkritische Untersuchungen zum Deuteronomium_. Bonn (Peter Hanstein), 1967.

Pritchard, James B., ed., <u>Ancient</u> <u>Near</u> <u>Eastern</u> <u>Texts</u> <u>Relating</u> <u>to</u> <u>the</u> <u>Old</u> <u>Testament</u>. 2nd. ed., Princeton (Princeton University Press), 1955.

Rabast, Karlheinz, <u>Das</u> <u>apodiktische</u> <u>Recht</u> <u>im</u> <u>Deuteronomium</u> <u>und</u> <u>im</u> <u>Heilig-keitsgesetz</u>. Berlin (Heimatdienstverlag), 1948.

Rad, Gerhard von, <u>Der</u> <u>Heilige</u> <u>Krieg</u> <u>im</u> <u>alten</u> <u>Israel</u>. Zürich, 1951.

_____, <u>Deuteronomy</u>: <u>A</u> <u>Commentary</u>. Philadelphia (Westminster), 1966.

_____, <u>Studies</u> <u>in</u> <u>Deuteronomy</u>. London (S. C. M. Press), 1953.

Rapaport, I., "The Origins of Hebrew Law." <u>PEQ</u>, (1941), 158-167.

Reiner, Erica, Šurpu: <u>A</u> <u>Collection</u> <u>of</u> <u>Sumerian</u> <u>and</u> <u>Akkadian</u> <u>Incantations</u>. Graz, 1958.

Rendtorff, R., <u>Die</u> <u>Gesetze</u> <u>in</u> <u>der</u> <u>Priesterschrift</u>. Göttingen (Vandenhoeck and Ruprecht), 1954.

_____, <u>Studien</u> <u>zur</u> <u>Geschichte</u> <u>des</u> <u>Opfers</u> <u>im</u> <u>alten</u> <u>Israel</u>. Neukirchen (Neukirchener Verlag), 1967.

Reventlow, H. G., <u>Das</u> <u>Heiligkeitsgesetz</u>: <u>Formgeschichtlich</u> <u>Untersucht</u>. Neukirchen (Neukirchener Verlag), 1961.

Richter, Wolfgang, <u>Recht</u> <u>und</u> <u>Ethos</u>. München (Kösel Verlag), 1966.

Rogers, R. W., <u>Cuneiform</u> <u>Parallels</u> <u>to</u> <u>the</u> <u>Old</u> <u>Testament</u>. New York, 1926.

Schmid, Hans Helmut, <u>Wesen</u> <u>und</u> <u>Geschichte</u> <u>der</u> <u>Weisheit</u>. <u>BZAW</u>, 101, Berlin (Töpelmann), 1966.

Smith, J. M. P., <u>The</u> <u>Origin</u> <u>and</u> <u>History</u> <u>of</u> <u>Hebrew</u> <u>Law</u>. Chicago (Chicago University Press), 1931.

Snaith, N. H., "Sacrifices in the Old Testament." <u>VT</u>, VII (1957), 315 ff.

Stamm, J. J., and M. E. Andrew, <u>The</u> <u>Ten</u> <u>Commandments</u> <u>in</u> <u>Recent</u> <u>Research</u>. Naperville (Alec R. Allenson), 1967.

Sturtevant, E. H., and G. Bechtel, <u>A</u> <u>Hittite</u> <u>Chrestomathy</u>. Philadelphia (Linguistic Society of America), 1935.

Thompson, R. Campbell, "Assyrian Prescriptions for Treating Bruises or Swellings." <u>American</u> <u>Journal</u> <u>of</u> <u>Semitic</u> <u>Languages</u> <u>and</u> <u>Literature</u>, XLVII (1930), 1-25.

Tilesse, G. Minette de, "Sections 'tu' et sections 'vous' dans le Deuteronome." <u>VT</u>. XII (1962), 29-87.

Vaux, Roland de, <u>Ancient</u> <u>Israel</u>: <u>Its</u> <u>Life</u> <u>and</u> <u>Institutions</u>. New York (McGraw-Hill), 1961.

Volten, Aksel, <u>Die</u> <u>moralischen</u> <u>Lehren</u> <u>des</u> <u>demotischen</u> <u>Papyri</u>, Louvre 2414 in <u>Studi</u> <u>in</u> <u>memoria</u> <u>di</u> <u>Ippol</u>. <u>Rosellini</u>. vol. II, Pisa, 1955.

Weinfeld, Moshe, "Cult Centralization in Israel in the Light of a Neo-Babylonian Analogy." <u>JNES</u>, XXIII (1964), 202-212.

_____, "The Origin of Humanism in Deuteronomy." <u>JBL</u>, LXXX (1961), 241-247.

_____, "The Provenance of Deuteronomy and the Deuteronomic School."
    unpub. diss., Jerusalem (Hebrew University), 1964.

Westermann, Claus, Basic Forms of Prophetic Speech. Philadelphia
    (Westminister), 1967.

Whitley, C. F., "Covenant and Commandment in Israel." JNES, XXII (1963),
    37-48.

Wilson, J. A., et. al., Authority and Law in the Ancient Orient. Supplements
    to Jaos, No. 17, 1954.

Wiseman, D. J., The Alalakh Tablets. London (British Institute of Archaeology
    at Ankara), 1953.

_____, "The Vassal Treaties of Esarhaddon." Iraq, XX (1958), 1-99.

REFERENCES

Chapter I

[1]The designation "If-You" is employed generally in this study to indicate conditional formulations using second person <u>singular</u> or <u>plural</u>.

[2]New York, 1897.

[3]<u>Ibid</u>., p. 242.

[4]<u>Die Genesis</u>, H.K.A.T., Div. I, Vol. I (Göttingen, 1901); <u>Ausgewählte Psalmen</u> (Göttingen, 1905) and <u>Einleitung in die Psalmen</u> ed. by J. Begrich, H.K.A.T., 2 vols. (Göttingen, 1928, 1933).

[5]"Die israelitische Literatur" in <u>Die Kultur der Gegenwart</u>, Div. I, Vol. VII, P. Hinneberg, ed. (Berlin, 1906), pp. 51-102.

[6]Göttingen, 1910, pp. 223-232, 238-241. See also <u>Die Schriften des Alten Testaments in Auswahl, neu übersetzt und für die Gegenwart erklärt</u> (Göttingen, 1914), p.229.

[7]Jirku, <u>Das weltliche Recht im Alten Testament: Stilgeschichtliche und rechtvergleichende Studien zu den juristischen Gesetzen des Pentateuchs</u> (Gütersloh, 1927). Jepsen, <u>Untersuchungen zum Bundesbuch</u> (Stuttgart, 1927).

[8]Paul Koschaker, <u>Quellenkritische Unterschungen zu den "altassyrische Gesetzen"</u> (Leipzig, 1921).

[9]<u>Op. cit</u>., pp. 32, 160.

[10]While Jirku recognized the close association of civil law and religious law in Israelite legislation, he wished on the other hand to make use of what he considered the objective and original separation between the two in his analysis, <u>ibid</u>., p. 10.

[11]<u>Ibid</u>., p. 37

[12]<u>Ibid</u>., p. 38.

[13]<u>Ibid</u>.

[14]<u>Ibid</u>., p. 39.

[15]<u>Ibid</u>., p. 40.

[16]<u>Ibid</u>.

[17]<u>Ibid</u>.

[18]<u>Ibid</u>., p. 41.

[19]<u>Ibid</u>., pp. 74f.

[20]<u>Ibid</u>., p. 41.

[21]Ibid., p. 42.

[22]In Sumerian the conditional is tukundi-bi, see A. Poebel, Grundzuge der sumerische Grammatik (Roestok, 1923), p. 423. In Akkadian it is šumma, see E. A. Speiser, "A Note on the Derivation of šumma," Journal of Cuneiform Studies, 1 (1947), pp. 321-328. In Hittite it is takku, see E. A. Hahn, "Some Hittite Works in ta-," Language, 12 (1936), pp. 109-113.

[23]ANET, pp. 167-168 (Nos. 36, 38, 39, 40, 187).

[24]ANET, pp. 191ff. (Nos. 48, 50, 51, 52, 54, 56, 167, 178, 181, 182, 183, 184, 185A and B, 186).

[25]Das Deuteronomium in der wissenschaftlichen Bearbeitung des 19. und 20. Jahrhunderts nebst 2 Anhängen Der Bericht 2 Kg. 22/23 und Die Stilgattung in den Gesetzen des Dtn. (Breslau, 1931).

[26]W. Staerk, Das Deuteronomium: sein Inhalt und seine literarische Form (Leipzig, 1894).

[27]K. Steuernagel, Der Rahmen des Deuteronomiums (Halle, 1894), and Die Entstehung des deuteronomischen Gesetzes (1896).

[28]Ibid., p. 26.

[29]Jirku, op. cit., pp. 74f.

[30]Krause, op. cit., p. 27. He omits vv. 2 and 3 from this group.

[31]Ibid. The conditional particle ʾim may be used in the statement of secondary cases.

[32]Ibid., p. 29. Here also the conditional particle ʾim may be used in the elaboration of the primary case.

[33]Ibid., p. 31.

[34]Ibid.

[35]Ibid., p. 32.

[36]Ibid., p. 35.

[37]Ibid., p. 36.

[38]Ibid., pp. 37f.

[39]Untersuchungen zum Bundesbuch (Stuttgart, 1927).

[40]Ibid., p. 55f.

[41]Ibid., pp. 82ff.

[42]Ibid., pp. 87ff.

[43]Ibid., p. 89.

[44]Ibid., p. 90.

[45]Ibid., pp. 95f.

[46]Le décalogue (Paris, 1927).

[47] Ibid., pp. 120ff.

[48] Ibid., p. 154.

[49] "The Book of the Covenant," Hebrew Union College Annual, 5 (1928), pp. 1-151; 7 (1930), pp. 10-258; 8-9 (1931-32), pp. 1-150, 741-6.

[50] Op. cit., Vol. 7, pp. 20ff.

[51] Ibid., pp. 31ff.

[52] Op. cit., Vol. 8-9, pp. 1ff.

[53] Ibid., p. 143.

[54] Op. cit., Vol. 7, p. 23.

[55] Die Ursprünge des israelitischen Rechts, (Leipzig, 1934) = Kleine Schriften I, pp. 278-332.

[56] In Alt's own words: "Sie beruht auf der Einsicht, dass in jeder einzelnen Literaturgattung, solange sie ihr eigenes Leben führt, bestimmte Inhalte mit bestimmten Ausdrucksformen fest verbunden und dass diese charac-teristischen Verbindungen, nicht etwa erst von Schriftstellern nachträglich und willkürlich den Stoffen aufgeprägt sind, sondern von jeher, also auch schon in der Frühzeit volksmässiger mündlicher Gestaltung und Überlieferung vor aller Literatur, wesenhaft zusammengehörten, da sie den besonderen, regelmässig wiederkehrenden Ereignissen und Bedürfnissen des Lebens ent-sprachen, aus denen die Gattungen je für sich erwuchsen." (Kleine Schriften I, p. 284).

[57] Ibid., pp. 285f.

[58] Ibid., pp. 288f.

[59] Ibid., p. 290.

[60] Ibid., p. 300.

[61] Ibid., pp. 303f.

[62] Ibid., p. 308.

[63] Ibid., p. 323.

[64] Ibid., p. 324.

[65] Ibid.

[66] Ibid., pp. 326-28.

[67] JBL, 55 (1936), 164-168, cf. also From the Stone Age to Christianity, pp. 267ff. Karlheinz Rabast, Das apodiktische Recht im Deuteronomiun und im Heiligkeitsgesetz (Berlin, 1948), has also employed Alt's theory.

[68] See the introductions of Eissfeldt, Weiser, Pfeiffer, and Bentzen.

[69] "Zur Geschichte des Dekalogs", ZAW 55 (1937), pp. 218-234.

[70] "Die babylonischen Termini für Gesetz und Recht," Symbolae Koschaker

126

(Leiden, 1939), p. 223, n. 19.

[71]"The Origins of Hebrew Law," PEQ, Oct. 1941, pp. 158-167.

[72]Hebrew Origins (New York, 1960, first pub. 1936), p. 72, see also ANET, p. 183, n. 24.

[73]"Ancient Oriental and Biblical Law," BA, 17 (1954), p. 30.

[74]Gunter Heinemann, "Untersuchungen zum apodiktischen Recht" (unpub. diss., Hamburg, 1958), has also noted the similarities between the Hittite treaties and the Old Testament covenant form and recognized apodictic forms in the treaties, but rather than a direct dependence, he prefers to see the Hittite form as having been mediated indirectly through the sanctuary of Baal Berith at Shechem. He also sees a similarity in the form of the Hittite treaties and the covenant renewal feast in Israel. Walter Beyerlin, Origins and History of the Oldest Sinaitic Traditions (Oxford, 1965), likewise acknowledges the correspondence between the formal elements of the Old Testament covenant form and that of the treaties (p. 54). However, he traces the origin of the Israelite covenant back to an earlier period when the people were encamped at Kadesh (pp. 145ff.). Here it was, he believes, that the covenant was first written down and deposited in some holy place.

[75]"West-Semitic Curses and the Problem of the Origins of Hebrew Law." VT, 2 (1961), pp. 137-158.

[76]"Apodiktisches und kasuistisches Recht im Licht agyptischer Analogien" Biblische Zeitschrift, 7 (1963), pp. 185-202.

[77]J. Begrich, "Die priesterliche Tora" BZAW, 66 (1936), pp. 63-88.

[78]Ibid., p. 73.

[79]An example is Lev. 11:8b.

[80]For example, Lev. 19:5.

[81]Begrich, op. cit., p. 75.

[82]Ibid.

[83]Examples are Lev. 11:4,5,6,7,8. (all plural).

[84]Begrich, op. cit., p. 76. An example is Lev. 7:27.

[85]Ibid., pp. 80ff.

[86]Etudes sur le Code de l'Alliance (Paris, 1946).

[87]Ibid., p. 109.

[88]Ibid., p. 110.

[89]Ibid., p. 117.

[90]Ibid., p. 110.

[91]Ibid., pp. 110f.

[92]Ibid., p. 112.

[93]Ibid.

[94] Ibid., p. 113.

[95] The Instructions of Ptah-hotep and the Instructions for Ka-Gemni.

[96] Op. cit., p. 114.

[97] Ibid., pp. 114, 126.

[98] Etudes, pp. 180f. In a later article, Cazelles seems to introduce a fifth category which he refers to as "declarative." See "Codigo de la Alianza" in Enciclopedia de la Biblia, Vol. 1 (Barcelona, Ediciones Garriga, I.A., 1963), pp. 362f. "La segunda seccion comienza en Ex. 22, 17 y se caracteriza por el estilo que se ha llamado 'apodictico,' pero que seria mejor llamar 'imperativo,' para no confundirlo con el estilo declarativo. Este, como en Esnunna, queda impersonal. . . ." (P. 362). No further reference is given.

[99] "The Forms of Israelite Law: A Comparative Study of Some Work Patterns in the Pentateuch" (unpub. diss., Rome, 1949), hereafter referred to as "The Forms." See also Two Forms of Israelite Law (Toronto, 1961).

[100] "The Forms,", p. 38.

[101] Ibid., p. 47. It seems strange to this writer that MacKenzie, having made such an observation, pursued it no further.

[102] Ibid., pp. 70ff.

[103] Ibid., p. 72.

[104] Ibid., p. 90. Rudolf Kilian, Literarkritische und Formgeschichtliche Untersuchung Des Heiligkeitsgesetzes (Bonn, 1963), has also posited an earlier origin for casuistic law than the period of the Conquest and the formation of the state (pp. 2f.).

[105] Ibid., p. 94.

[106] Ibid., pp. 96f.

[107] Ibid., p. 99.

[108] Ibid., pp. 100f.

[109] Ibid., p. 109.

[110] Ibid., p. 111.

[111] Alt, op. cit., p. 308.

[112] MacKenzie, "The Forms", p. 112.

[113] The first and the last of the twelve curses (v. 15 and v. 26) are in relative form.

[114] "The Forms", p. 124.

[115] Ibid., p. 127.

[116] Jirku had separated the singular and plural forms in his analysis, op. cit., p. 41.

[117] Ibid., pp. 134f.

128

[118] _Ibid._, p. 144.

[119] _Ibid._, p. 145.

[120] _Ibid._, p. 154.

[121] _Ibid._, p. 155.

[122] _Ibid._, p. 162.

[123] The following reflect conditions of a settled way of life: Exod. 23:19, Deut. 19:14a, 22:9-10, Lev. 2:1, 4,5,7,14, Deut. 17:14f., 22:8, 23:25f., 24:10-13, 24:s9, 20, 21.

[124] Walter Kornfeld, _Studien zum Heiligkeitsgesetz_ (Wien, 1952), has adopted MacKenzie's classification with little modification.

[125] _Untersuchungen zum Heiligkeitsgesetz_ (Berlin, 1964).

[126] _Ibid._, p. 121.

[127] _Ibid._, p. 126.

[128] "Beobachtungen zum Stil alttestamentlicher Rechtssätze, "_Theologische Litaeraturzeitung_, 85 (1960), col. 147-150.

[129] _Ibid._, col. 150.

[130] _Wesen und Herkunft des 'apodiktischen Rechts'_ (Neukrichen, 1965). See also his "Covenant and Commandment,"_JBL_, 84 (1965), pp. 38-51.

[131] _Ibid._, p. 23.

[132] See above, pp. 18-19.

[133] _Op. cit._, p. 27.

[134] _Ibid._, p. 35.

[135] _Ibid._, pp. 28ff.

[136] _Ibid._, p. 89

[137] _Ibid._, pp. 77ff.

[138] _Ibid._, pp. 96ff.

[139] _Ibid._, pp. 117ff.

[140] _Ibid._, pp. 141ff.

[141]Fohrer, "Das sogenannte apodiktisch formulierte Recht und der Dakalog, "Kerygma und Dogma, 2 (1965), pp. 49-74, Richter. Recht und Ethos (Munich, 1966). Hans Jochen Boecker, Redeformen des Rechtsleben im Alten Testament (Neukirchen, 1964), has also disputed the cultic origin of the participial laws.

[142]In a review of Richter's study, JBL, 86 (1967), pp. 489-91, Gerstenberger notes that the former's account of the different backgrounds of the prohibitive and vetitive forms is imprecise.

Chapter II

[1]Also included in this category are the narrative portions of the prophetic books.

[2]In the following analysis the term "imperative" is used broadly to refer to formulations which may or may not be formulated with the grammatical imperative. Whenever the grammatical imperative is intended, it is so stated.

[3]Jud. 6:17, I Sam. 27:5 and Neh. 2:5.

[4]Gen. 31:44.

[5]Cuthbert A. Simpson, "Genesis: Exegesis," IB, vol. I, p. 716.

[6]E. A. Speiser, Genesis: The Anchor Bible (New York, 1964), p. 249.

[7]II Chr. 18:27 = Kgs. 22:28.

[8]See BDB, p. 473, par. 2b; 'im with imperfect implies possibility, see Gesenius, et. al., Hebrew Grammar, pp. 494f.

[9]I Kgs. 3:14, 6:12, 9:4-7, 11:38.

[10]Read with LXX.

[11]II Ch. 10:6f. - I Kgs. 12:6f.

[12]Read with LXX.

[13]For example, in Jud. 16:13b and in I Sam. 19:11b.

[14]For example, in II Ch. 25:7f. and Esther 4:14.

[15]Claus Westermann, Basic Forms of Prophetic Speech (Philadelphia, 1967), p. 90, trans. of Grundformen prophetischer Rede, Chr. Kaiser Verlag, Munich.

[16]L. Köhler, "Formen und Stoffe," Deuterojesaja, stilkritisch untersucht (Giessen, 1923), pp. 102-105; J. Lindblom, Die literarische Gattung der prophetischen Literatur (Uppsala, 1924). See also Westermann, op. cit., pp. 98ff.

[17]It is quite possible, of course, that the prophet's will may become one with that of Yahweh; however, the frequent unwillingness of the prophets to declare the message of Yahweh certainly militates against a one-for one identification of the will of the prophet with that of Yahweh.

[18]Isa. 58:13f., Jer. 17:24, 17:17.

[19]Jer. 7:5-7, 22:4f.

[20]Jer. 42:10, 13-15.

[21]Isa. 1:19f.

[22]Jer. 13:17.

[23]Jer. 4:1.

[24]Isa. 7:9b, Jer. 22:4f.

[25]Jer. 42:10, 13-15.

[26]Mal. 2:2.

[27]Zec. 3:7.

[28]There is a single exception to this pattern. In Jer. 4:1 there are actually two If-You formulations. The apodosis of the first contains a demand, and in this respect it is like the two exceptions in narratives, Jos. 24:15 and I Sam. 7:3.

[29]Op. cit., p. 98.

[30]J. Hempel appears to have first differentiated the exhortation as an expansion in Die althebräische Literatur und ihr hellenistisch-judisches Nachleben (Potsdam, 1934), pp. 56-68.

[31]See G. Hölscher, Die Propheten (Leipzig, 1914), p. 382, R.H. Pfeiffer, Introduction to the Old Testament (New York, 1941), pp. 504ff.

[32]See below p. 172.

[33]The term "proverb" is intentionally avoided since it is commonly employed in a more general sense which would include under it other forms such as the counsel.

[34]Qoheleth after all is only a title, not a proper name.

[35]See ANET, pp. 412-21, 427f.; also Prov. 1:8, 2:1, 3:1, Eccles. 11:12, Tobit 4:5ff., Sirach 2:1, 3:1.

[36]See Deut. 6:7.

[37]The same is probably also the case with regard to a prophet and his disciples.

Chapter III

[1] C.H. Cornill, Einleitung in das Alte Testament (Tübingen, 1891), Translated by G.H. Box, Introduction to the Canonical Books of the Old Testament (London, 1907).

[2] K. Steuernagel, Der Rahmen des Deuteronomiums (Halle, 1894). W. Staerk, Das Deuteronomium: sein Inhalt und seine literarische Form (Leipzig, 1894). Both of these works were unavailable to the writer. For a discussion, see George Adam Smith, The Book of Deuteronomy (Cambridge, 1918), pp. LXXIIIf.

[3] So Staerk; also Johannes Hempel, Die Schichten des Deuteronomiums (Leipzig, 1914), pp. 104ff., and Otto Eissfeldt, The Old Testament: An Introduction (New York, 1965), pp. 226ff.

[4] So Steuernagel, op. cit.

[5] So F. Horst, Das Privilegrecht Jahwes (Göttingen, 1930)=Gesammelte Studien (Munich, 1961) pp. 17-154, who concluded that underlying the D code was an original pre-Deuteronomic decalogue whichhad been expanded through three successive editions. Horst suggested a twofold process of composition of Deuteronomy, first by Levites of North Israel, whose work was brought to Jerusalem and subsequently taken up and developed there by a Wisdom school. RGG, II, 3rd. ed., p. 102. H.H. Hospers, De numerusivisseling in het boek Deuteronomium (diss. Utrecht, 1942), unavailable to the writer. Gerhard von Rad, Studies in Deuteronomy (London, 1953), p. 11, also in his more recent article "Deuteronomy" in IDB, vol. I (Nashville, 1962), p. 832.

[6] G. Minette de Tilesse, "Sections 'tu' et sections 'vous' dans le Deuteronome", VT 12 (1962), pp. 29-87.

[7] Henri Cazelles, "Passages in the Singular Within Discourse in the Plural of Dt. 1-4", CBQ 29 (1967), pp. 207-219.

[8] Martin Noth, Überlieferungsgeschichtliche Studien I (Tübingen, 1957), pp. 16ff.

[9] The term "preceptive" is used herein to refer to the laws in You-Shall style. It will be shown in the following analysis that the great majority of laws in If-You style also belong to this category.

[10] "The Forms", p. 127.

[11] The following abbreviations are employed: BC-Book of the Covenant, HC - Holiness Code, D - Deuteronomy, J- Yahwist source, P - priestly source.

[12] Jepsen, op. cit., pp. 55ff.; also Alt, op. cit., pp. 303f.

[13] B. Gemser, "The Importance of the Motive Clause in Old Testament Law" in Supplements to Vetus Testamentum I (Copenhagen, 1953), pp. 50-66.

[14] Studies in Deuteronomy, p. 16.

[15] Similarly Martin Noth, Leviticus: A Commentary (Philadelphia, 1965), P. 144.

[16] Ibid., p. 187.

[17] See Ibid., p. 189.

[18] See below, pp. 150 f.

[19] Julius Wellhausen, Prolegomena zur Geschichte Israels (1883), E.T. Prolegomena to the History of Ancient Israel, pp. 402, ff.; also J. M. P. Smith, The Origin and History of Hebrew Law (Chicago, 1931), p. 44; and R.H. Pfeiffer, Introduction to the Old Testament (New York, 1941), pp. 179f.

[20] "The Origin of Humanism in Deuteronomy", JBL 80 (1961), pp. 241-247.

[21] "The Forms", p. 159.

[22] See below, p. 144.

[23] R. H. Pfeiffer, op. cit., p. 221, traces the ritual decalogue back to Canaanite practice.

[24] Roland de Vaux, Ancient Israel: Its Life and Institutions (New York, 1961), p. 444.

[25] See Lev. 11:1 ff. and Deut. 14:4 ff.

[26] M. Noth holds that 34:20 is the original because of the shorter composition of ch. 34 as compared to ch. 13, Exodus: A Commentary (Philadelphia, 1962), p. 263.

[27] G. B. Gray, Sacrifice in the Old Testament (Oxford, 1925), pp. 114ff.

[28] See Jud. 6:20, 13:19.

[29] Helmer Ringgren, Israelite Religion (Philadelphia, 1966), p. 25.

[30] Yohannan Aharoni, "Arad: Its Inscriptions and Temple", Biblical Archaeologist 31 (Feb. 1968), p. 19.

[31] I Kgs. 8:64, II Kgs. 16:14.

[32] For the second Temple see I Macc. 4:45; also Flavius Josephus, Contra Apion I, 22, quoting Hecataeus. For the third Temple, see Josephus, Wars of the Jews V., 56. also Mishnah, Mid. 34.

[33] Gray, op. cit., p. 127

[34] The word מנחה probably always indicated a gift of grain or cereal. But since the basic meaning of the word is "tribute" or "gift" , it was applied more widely and could refer to the whole ceremony. See N.H. Snaith, "Sacrifices in the Old Testament", VT 7 (1957), p. 315.

[35]Rolf Rendtorff, _Die Gesetze in der Priesterschrift_ (Göttingen, 1954),
P. 20. He has argued for a distinction within Begrich's priestly dā'āt,
which he names Ritual (ritual prescription), present in Lev. 1-5. In contrast to the usual priestly dā'āt, he believes this ritual formulation was
intended for public recital. See also Rendtorff, _Studien zur Geschichte
des Opfers im alten Israel_ (Neukirchen, 1967), p. 182, in which he reit-
erates this position.

[36]Klaus Koch, _Die Priesterschrift von Exodus 25 bis Leviticus 16_
(Göttingen, 1959), p. 51. Koch, closely following Rendtorff, also recognizes a ritual form behind Lev. 1-5. He differs with the latter in his
analysis of the exact scheme of the supposed ritual.

[37]Karl Elliger, _Leviticus_, HZAT, 4 (Tübingen, 1966), pp. 30 ff. Elliger
believes Lev. 2 stems from the same circles as Lev. 1, 3-5, but was not composed at the same time (p. 43).

[38]For example, Lev. 1:1 f., 7:22 f., 7:26, 7:32, 11:1f.

[39]_Der Heilige Krieg im alten Israel_ (Zürich, 1951, reprinted Göttingen,
1958), also _Studies in Deuteronomy_, pp. 45ff. and _Deuteronomy: A Commentary_,
pp. 25ff.

[40]Based partly on von Rad's analysis, _Der Heilige Krieg_, pp. 6ff.

[41]The only exception is Deut. 20:10f.

[42]See also 19:1ff., 21:2ff.

[43]The presence of priests with the army is attested for example in
Num. 31:6 and I Sam. 4:4.

[44]_Deuteronomy: A Commentary_, p. 131.

[45]E.g., Josh. 8:1.

[46]The term appears to be derived from the Addadian _šatāru_ which means
"to write"; see BDB, p. 1009. The term _šōterim_ thus appears to indicate
officials whose duties included clerical responsibilities and record keeping.
This interpretation is supported by II Chr. 26:11; see also Weinfeld, "The
Provenance of Deuteronomy and the Deuteronomic School." unpub. diss.
Jerusalem (Hebrew Univeristy), 1964, hereinafter referred to as "Provenance".

[47]The Heb. reads יְחַלְּלֶנּוּ וְלֹא , lit. "and not profane it".

[48]So von Rad, _Deuteronomy: A Commentary_, p. 132; also F. Schwally
Semitische Kriegsaltertumer, (Leipzig, 1901), pp. 75ff.

[49]ANET, p. 48.

[50]Krause, _op. cit._, p. 26.

134

[51] Jirku's contention that the deferment regulations were originally formulated in If-You style is without adequate foundation; see op. cit., pp. 74f.

[52] Similarly von Rad, Deuteronomy: A Commentary, pp. 132f.

[53] II Kgs. 7:12, I Kgs. 20:1f., II Sam. 11:1, I Kgs. 16:15f.

[54] The boast of Tiglath Pileser III: cp. II Kgs. 3:16-19.

[55] Reading ◻ 𝗍 𝗑 𝗍 for ◻ 𝗍 𝗑 𝗍 with the LXX.

[56] Similarly von Rad, Deuteronomy, p. 137.

[57] I, n.8 and 75, cf. RB, 66 (1959), p. 576.

[58] Cp. Num. 5:1-4.

[59] An example is the "Military Instructions of the Hittite King Tuthaliya IV", Sedat Alp. op. cit., pp. 403ff.

[60] See Exod. 23:6-8, Deut. 21:18-21, 22:18-19.

[61] So M. Noth, Exodus, p. 180.

[62] Alt, Kleine Schriften I, pp. 341ff., has noted that the style of this insertion may derive from liturgical usage.

[63] Deut. 17:7, 17:12, 19:13, 19:19, 21:9, 21:21, 22:21, 22:22, 22:24, 24:7.

[64] See Deut. 17:7.

[65] Weinfeld has suggested that the magistrates in Deuteronomy are identical with the army officers, "Provenance," footnotes p. 106. See also J. Naveh, "A Hebrew Letter from the Seventh Century B.C., " IEJ 10 (1960), pp. 129-139.

[66] See II Sam. 12:1-6, 14:1-11, I Kgs. 3:16-28, 7:7, II Kgs. 4:13, 15:5, Prov. 20:8.

[67] ANET., p. 149.

[68] ANET., p. 151.

[69] D. J. Wiseman, The Alalakh Tablets, Nos. 17 and 101.

[70] ANET, p. 184 par. 47, and p. 195, par. 173.

[71] See M. Greenberg, "City of Refuge." IDB, vol. I. p.638f.

[72] ANET., p. 167, par. 24.

[73] ANET., p. 189, par. 6.

[74] See Deut. 16:18 and 17:9.

[75] Jos. 8:29, 10:26, I Sam. 31:10, II Sam. 4:12.

[76] Similarly Weinfeld, "Provenance", p. 205.

[77] Deut. 21:19-21, 22:15ff., 25:8-9.

[78] Deut. 19:12.

[79] Deut. 21:1-9.

[80] See 22:15, 18, 21.

[81] Weinfeld, "Provenance," p. 132, considers these matters to have been under the jurisdiction of the judges.

[82] ANET.,p. 181, tab. A, par. 8.

[83] A criminal offence is one involving a wrong committed against society and punished by society. Such offences threaten the well-being of the Society itself in distinction from disputes between individuals which are of a private nature and which are usually settled by arbitration.

[84] For example: homicide (Ex. 21:12, Lev. 24:21b), religious crimes (Ex. 22:19, 31:14b, 14c, Lev. 24:16a), sexual offences (Ex. 22:18, Deut. 27:20-23).

[85] See also Deut. 21:18-21, which seems to be a rationalization of the patria potestas.

[86] See also Lev. 19:15.

[87] See below p. 153.

[88] See above, p. 59, n. 8.

[89] S. R. Driver, A Critical and Exegetical Commentary on Deuteronomy, The International Critical Commentary (New York, 1895), pp. ixxvii ff., see also Johannes Hempel, Die Schichten des Deuteronomiums (Leipzig, 1914), pp. 103ff., and Ludwig Köhler, Die hebraische Rechtsgemeinde, Jahresbericht der Universität Zürich (Zürich, 1930-31), pp. 17f.

[90] Von Rad, Studies, pp. 14ff.

[91] Ibid., p. 16.

[92] O Bächli, Israel und kie Volker:eine Studie zum Deuteronomium (Zürich, 1962), pp. 186ff.

136

[93] E. W. Nicholson, Deuteronomy and Tradition (Philadelphia, 1967), p. 101.

[94] Weinfeld, "Provanance"; see also his more recent article "Deuteronomy - The Present State of Inquiry", JBL 86 (1967), p. 262.

[95] Driver, op. cit., p. lxxxv.

[96] See above p. 101.

[97] Deut. 8:19, 11:13, 11:22, 28:1; also Exod. 15:26, 19:5f., and 23:22.

[98] Von Rad tacitly admits that there are differences between the parenetic styles of these two bodies of law, Studies, p. 36.

Chapter IV

[1] Cf. Cazelles, op. cit., p. 114; also Christa Kayatz, Studien zu Proverbien 1-9 (Neukirchen, 1966), pp. 26ff.

[2] See Erica Reiner, Šurpu (Graz, 1958), p. 11; ANET. p. 334 ("Ritual to be Followed by the Kalu-Priest when Covering the Temple Kettle-Drum"); ANET, p. 339 ("Ritual for the Repair of a Temple"); and ANET, p. 357 (Ritual for the Erection of a New Palace").

[3] The existence of other kinds of wisdom is here upheld. Cf. J. L. Crenshaw, "Method in Determining Wisdom Influence upon 'Historical' Literature," JBL, 88, pp. 129ff.

[4] At least two sculptures of such scribes have come to light both dating from ca. 2500 B.C.; cf. J. B. Pritchard, The Ancient Near East in Pictures (Princeton, 1954), p. 40.

[5] Cf. ANET, "The Satire on Trades," pp. 432-35.

[6] They are: "The Instruction of the Vizier Ptah-hotep," "The Instruction for King Meri-ka-re," "The Instruction of King Amen-em-het," "The Instruction of Cheti the Scribe, the Son of Duauf," "The Instruction of Ani," "The Instruction of Amen-em-ope," "Papyrus Insinger," "The Instruction of 'Onchsheshonqy"; fragentarily preserved are: "The Instruction for Ka-gemni" and "The Instruction of Hor-dedef."

[7] See R. W. Rogers, Cuneiform Parallels to the Old Testament (New York, 1926), pp. 175-178; also ANET, pp. 426f. W. G. Lambert, "Babylonian Moral Teachings" in Documents From Old Testament Times, ed. by D. Winton Thomas (New York, 1958), p. 104, believes the work is a product of the Cassite Period, 1500-1000 B.C.

[8] ANET, pp. 427-430. While the writing was found at Elephantine, A.E. Goodman holds that the actual provenance is Assyria and that it tells of events which happened during the reign of Sennacherib, "The Words of Ahikar" in Documents From Old Testament Times, ed. by E. Winton Thomas, p. 270.

[9] ANET, p. 415.

[10] ANET, p. 421.

[11] Glanville, Catalogue of Demotic Papyri in the British Museum, Vol.II, The Instruction of 'Onchsheshonqy Part I (London, 1955), p. xii.

[12] Ibid.

[13] I purposely avoid the usual designation "instruction" in order to avoid confusion with my own categories.

[14] "Instructions for Palace Personnel to Insure the King's Purity," trans. by Albrecht Goetze, ANET, p. 207.

[15] "Instructions for Temple Officials, " trans. by Albrecht Goetze, ANET, pp. 207-210.

[16] "Military Instructions of the Hittite King Tuthaliya IV" by Sedat Alp, Beleten 11 (1947), pp. 383-414; also "From the Instructions for the Commander of the Border Guard," ANET, p. 210f., not in If-You style.

[17] See Herbert Liebesny, "The Administration of Justice in Nuzi", JAOS 63 (1943), pp. 128-144.

[18] Ibid., p. 129.

[19] Reproduced by S. N. Kramer in The Sumerians: Their History, Culture, and Character (Chicago, 1963), pp. 340-342.

[20] R. Campbell Thompson, "Assyrian Prescriptions For Treating Bruises or Swellings" , American Journal of Semitic Languages and Literature, XLVII (Oct. 1930) No. 1, pp. 1-25, and "The Installation of the Vizier" in the Tomb of Rekhmi-re at Thebes, vol. I, ed. by Norman de Garis Davies (New York, 1948), pp. 86f.

[21] ANET, p. 210.

[22] See the example above, p.155.

[23] ANET, p. 208.

[24] ANET, p. 207.

[25] G. E. Mendenhall, "Covenant Forms in Israelite Tradition, "BA XVII (Sept. 1954) No. 3. He isolates six basic elements in the treaties: 1) Preamble, 2) The Historical Prologue, 3) The Stipulations, 4) provision for the deposit in the temple and periodic public reading, 5) list of gods as witnesses, and 6) the curses and blessings formula. See also Mendenhall, "Covenant, " IDB, vol. 1, pp. 714-723.

[26] An extensive bibliography can be found in D.J. McCarthy, Treaty and Covenant (Rome, 1963), pp. xiii f.

138

[27] Erhard Gerstenberger, "Covenant and Commandment," JBL, 84 (1965), pp. 38-51.

[28] Esarhaddon with Ramataia of Urakazabanu (D.J. Wiseman, The Vassal Treaties of Esarhaddon), Esarhaddon with Baal of Tyre (R. Borger, Inschriften Asarhaddons) Ashurnirari V with Mati 'ilu of Bit-Agusi (E. Weidner, Archiv für Orientforschung, vol. 8), Niqmepa, king of Mukis and Alalakh with Ir-im, king of Tunis, (D.J. Wiseman, The Alalakh Tablets) Bar-ga'-ayah of KTK with Mati'el of Arpad (A. Dupont-Sommer, Les Inscriptions arameennes de Sfire) Huqqanas (Keilschrifttexte aus Boghazkoi, vol. 4), Mursilis II with Manapa-Dattas (Keilschrifttexte aus Boghazkoi, vol. 4), Muwatallis with Alaksandus (Keilschrifttexte aus Boghazkoi, vol. 4), Mursilis II with Niqmepa of Ugarit (J. Nougayrol, Palais royal d'Ugarit IV), Tudhaliyas IV with Ulmi-Teshub of Dattasa (Keilschrifttexte aus Boghazkoi, vol. 4), Mursilis with Duppi-Teshub of Amurru (ANET), Suppiluliumas with Mattiwaza (ANET).

[29] See ANET, pp. 201-203

[30] Wiseman, The Alalakh Tablets, (London, 1953), p. 29.

[31] ANET, p. 204, 1.11.

[32] ANET, p. 206.

[33] ANET, p. 205.

Chapter V

[1] See above p. 146.

[2] Ibid.

[3] See Num. 18:26, addressed to the Levites.

[4] See Pfeiffer, op, cit., pp. 504f.

[5] ANET, p. 208, "Instructions to Temple Officials," i, 45ff.

[6] See also Prov. 6:23, 7:2.

[7] Ptah-hotep.

[8] 'Onchsheshonqy.

[9] Klostermann held that the parenetic style stemmed from public reciters of the law [Der Pentateuch (1907), pp. 154ff.] ; Bentzen regarded Levitical instructors of the law as responsible [Die Josianische Reform und ihre Vorausset-zungen (1926)], as did also von Rad [Studies. pp. 14ff]; Weiser regarded it as cultic in origin [The Old Testament: Its Formation and Development (1961), pp. 126ff.].

[10] Bächli, op. cit., pp. 88f.

[11] Weinfeld, "Provenance", pp. 10-69.

[12] Nicholson, op. cit., p. 101.

[13] Elements of humanitarian morality are also found in the "Instruction for King Meri-ka-re", the "Instruction of King Amen-em-het", the "Prophecy of Nefer-Rohu", the "Admonitions of Ipu-Wer", the "Protest of the Eloquent Peasant", and the declarations of innocence in the Book of the Dead.

[14] ANET, p. 149.

[15] ANET, p. 151.

[16] E.g., see the "Inscription of Azitawadda of Adana" and the Inscription of Kilamuwa of Y'dy-Sam'al", ANET, pp. 500f.

[17] See F. Charles Fensham, "Widow, Orphan, and the Poor in Ancient Near Eastern Legal and Wisdom Literature" JNES 21 (1962), p. 138.

[18] See Roland de Vaux, Ancient Israel: Its Life and Institutions (New York, 1961), p. 11; also Morroe Berger, The Arab World Today (New York, 1964) pp. 47ff.

[19] See von Rad, Studies in Deuteronomy, pp. 45ff. and Der Heilige Krieg im alten Israel, pp. 68ff.

[20] See I Sam. 9:16, 10:1.

[21] See Weinfeld, "Deuteronomy - The Present State of Inquiry", JBL 86 (1967), p. 256.

[22] See I. Mendelsohn, "Authority and Law in Canaan-Israel" in Authority and Law in the Ancient Orient JAOS Supp. No. 17, 1954, pp. 25f. "In the Keret Legend we are told that the king once invited his seventy "bulls" (translated "peers"), and his eighty "gazelles" (translated "barons"), to a feast. The text does not inform us about the functions of those "peers" and "barons". But from similar references in the Old Testament to the "oxen of Edom," "the rams of Moab, " and "the he-goats of the land," it is quite clear that Keret's "bulls" and "gazelles" were the representatives of the aristocracy who in some way shared in the government of the kingdom of Ugarit.
Rib-Addi, an Egyptian official in the el-Amarna period, mentions "the city lords" of Byblos. Prince Zaker-Baal of the same city (ca. 1100 B.C.) convened his city-council, the mô'ēd, in order to decide the fate of the unfortunate Egyptian envoy Wen-Amon. The term "lords of the city," which was applied by Rib-Addi to the aristocracy of Byblos, is employed also to designate the oligarchy of Shechem. It was the ba'alē shekhem who gave Abimelek seventy pieces of silver to carry on the war against his half-brothers.

[23] See Judg. 9:6; I Sam. 8:4-5; II Sam. 3:17, 5:3.

[24] See I Kgs. 21:8ff; II Kgs. 10:1ff.; Dt. 19:12.

*296=6
5-08
CC

Q*992*9
S-08
CC